gorilla architecture

GORILLA ARCHITECTURE

selected poems by CARL MILLER DANIELS

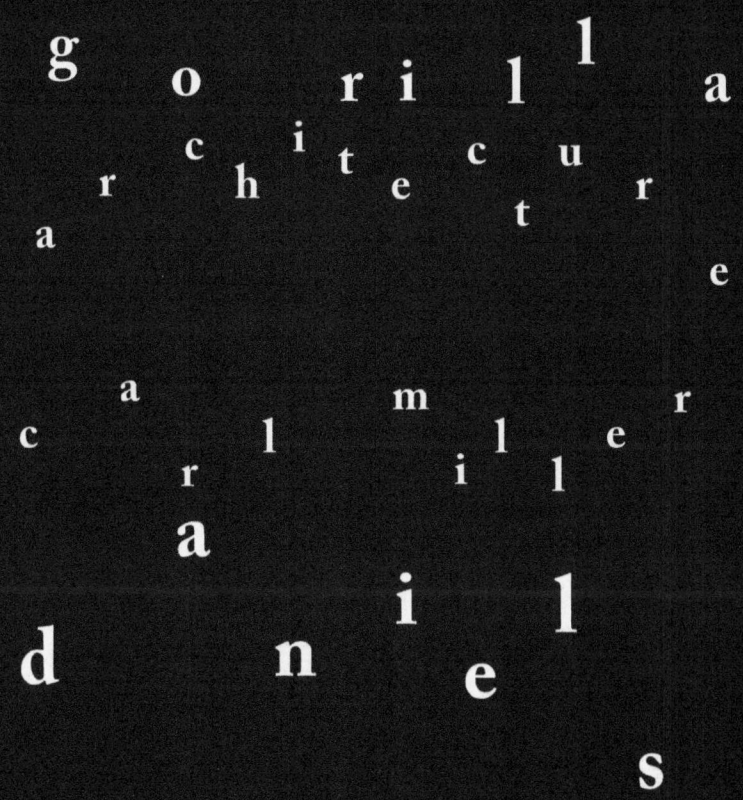

INTERIOR NOISE PRESS
Austin, TX

Gorilla Architecture
Copyright © 2011 by Carl Miller Daniels

All rights reserved. Printed in the United States of America. No part of this book may be used or reproduced in any manner whatsoever without written permission except in the case of brief quotations embodied in critical articles and reviews.

For order information and current mailing address please visit www.interiornoisepress.com

Interior Noise Press
Austin, TX

Cover Photograph by Jon Miller
Book Design by David p Bates

Library of Congress Control Number: 2011938394

ISBN 978-0-9816606-2-2
First Edition

*Dedicated to
pickle relish–
and
Serious Literature*

contents

half-light of whiskey science	15
thread	16
critical acclaim	18
a few mean minutes	19
sprocket	20
slower, yes, much more slowly than that	22
scooter	23
greenpussysprouts	24
butterflies and sirloin	26
so how was your vacation?	28
lagomorphic medicine	29
experiencing any discomfort	30
how many prawns can you eat?	31
the patriot	33
great expectations, marvelous	34
bow wow	36
brillo pads	37
water beans	39
nests	41
specializing in art history	43
DNA	46
hero parsnips with succotash	48
black n' white linoleum	49

when it works	50
fluorescent mangos	51
a while ago	52
equals	53
ceremony	54
weenies	55
vernal	56
a bit of whimsy for the susceptible proofilites	57
the pangs of separation	60
brushwork	61
radishes are red, too	62
again	63
ozone	64
sore	66
a life in whispers	68
nocturnal bio boy vs. the algebraic blues	69
review	71
pissing on potted plants	72
different	74
lawrence	76
can't hear you	77
pop goes the weasel	79
undomesticated	81

phantoms	83
at the molecular level	85
14-hour drive	87
tendon	89
vergil died 19 B.C.– and scott's pecs	91
degree	93
wrestling with change	95
shopping list, folded in the middle	97
early winter	98
twist & shout	100
slide over	102
sherwin-williams	104
enter at your own risk	106
growth rings	108
all quiet	110
the sensation of really thick bread mold	112
90% clean	113
what if	115
pragmatically speaking, guava jellies stain	116
a job	117
beans	118
bipolar stadium	122
whimpersville	123

my money's on the t-shirt he keeps under the front seat	125
squid fuckers	127
suddenly! grabbed by nostalgia!	130
too beautiful	135
pure pleasure, thematic musings, beautiful male flesh	136
sardines	138
first love	139
next to the rope burn	141
twice the size of our regular brand	142
working through it	144

I have never yet enjoyed a day, but I have never stopped trying to arrange for happiness.

Jane Bowles

It's not what you see that is art; art is the gap.

Maracel Duchamp

half-light of whiskey science

the hens in the henhouse smell scratchy and rough to
me, as i go through the nests and extract the eggs.
my grandmother has taught me how to do this, but
now, i am on my own. she trusts me. i am what,
7, 8, 9 years old? maybe younger than that.
maybe older. memories blur and fuzz and
perhaps even grow soft downy feathers
as one gets older. i remember the odor,
though, of the henhouse. the odor was
dark, and musky, and, yes, female. broodish.
perhaps the eggs themselves had no aroma.
perhaps it was just the aura of the henhouse
itself. or, perhaps, still warm from the body
heat of the chickens, the eggs smelled of
the female body parts they had just passed
through on their way to the nest, on their
way to my hands, and then into the waiting basket
into which i placed them. i carried
the warm eggs back to my grandmother, there
in her kitchen, where she washed
them gently with a soft brush in the sink;
she may have used a little dish-washing
soap on them, too, but i just can't remember
that part. then, she dried them off
and put them in a big white bowl
in the refrigerator,
where they became cold, and quite
odorless, as if there never had been
any odor, ever– and, if there had been, we
just wouldn't think about it anymore.

thread

from the steering wheel dangled the lips
of a dead dog. the lips were beef-jerky
in texture, and they dangled at the end of a string.
**

the driver of the car was a sexy naked young
man, with a big scar on the outer thigh
of his right leg. his big dick was
hard as a rock as he drove the
car into his driveway, and climbed
out onto the hot pavement, at just about
midnight.
**

he didn't act like he cared one way
or the other if anyone saw
him in all his big-dicked
nakedness as he climbed
out of the car. quite
matter-of-factly, he unlocked
the front door to his house
and walked inside. he
gently closed the door behind him.
**

the interior of the house
was immaculate. tidy clean.
no dust. he walked around
in there wagging his big
hard dick and exploring
the texture of the scar
on his thigh with
the fingertips of his
right hand.
**

standing
naked in front of the refrigerator,
he dreamed of
fixing himself a big thick
steak, but settled

on a tub of cottage cheese,
instead.
**

the dog lips that dangled
from the steering wheel
he had removed
from a dead dog that
he'd found lying beside
a back-country road
a few weeks ago. they
had mummified nicely,
and, now, just when
he wanted to eat
cottage cheese and jerk himself
off, he could hear those damn
rubbery dog lips telling
him to put on his pajamas
and just go to bed and
go directly to sleep.
he flew into a rage
and tossed the
tub of cottage cheese
up against the kitchen
wall. he spent the
rest of the night
cleaning the kitchen,
so that, by morning,
it was even more immaculate
than it had started out.
**

standing in the shower,
his big dick hard and throbbing,
he resisted the urge
to jerk off, and
told himself, once again,
that those goddamn dog lips,
just had
to go.

critical acclaim

into the lagoon plunged the sexy naked young man,
but THE CREATURE grabbed him,
there in the black water.
then, quite suddenly,
the sexy naked young man and THE CREATURE
were hugging each other, desperate for
the love they'd so often been denied
during the course
of their furtive and disparate lives.
they clambered up onto a small island
there in the middle of the lagoon,
and then they told each other their sadnesses
and their sorrows. again, they hugged
affectionately. they were both at peace now,
but, still, just a tad bit wary of
overly earnest
erections.

a few mean minutes

he sat there clipping his nails—
first the fingernails, then
the toenails. he was
sitting on a bench in the
locker room of the college gymnasium,
and his nail trimmings
fell onto the floor.
this was a rude gesture, and he
knew it. leaving his nail
trimmings there on the
floor for anyone to step on. he sat
there sexy and good-looking and
naked on the locker room bench,
clipping his nails, his
fingernails, and his toenails,
too. he left the little pile
of nail trimmings there on the floor, and
he walked naked into the showers.
no one around. still no one
around. he showered and
shampooed, returned
to his locker, saw the
little pile of
trimmings there in front
of his locker, and still no one
was around. he sighed,
dressed, and walked outside
into the daylight. then, he
spat onto the sidewalk,
and, all things considered,
he did it again.

sprocket

the sexy pan-sexual boy spurted
a heck of a lot of cum.
once, when he was just
sitting there at his own
desk in his own bedroom,
minding his own business, reading
a novel he had been
assigned to read by his
English teacher,
the sexy pan-sexual boy got
a hardon and spurted cum
immediately, with his pants
still on. the sexy pan-sexual boy
sat there with the cum
spot on the front of his pants,
and he
thought about life, and about
spurting cum, and he thought
about reading books,
and he thought about spurting
cum. then, he stood up
from his desk and
stripped off his pants and
stripped off his underpants
and then heck the rest of
it, too, all the clothes,
and
the sexy pan-sexual boy
stood there naked,
so naked that
the little hairs
on the inside of his
ankles
fluttered like shy
butterflies, and
several of them actually
took flight

and landed
on the ceiling,
and then watched him,
as he stood there
down below,
looking up.

slower, yes, much more slowly than that

i thought nothing of squirrel's breath coming out of
my ears as i stood
naked in the dark in the hallway outside
the bedroom of my sexy college roommate,
him a swimmer on the swimteam, sexy guy,
i was wild about him, delirious nearly,
me just a skinny blond guy majoring
in biology and minoring in english,
him majoring in electrical engineering
and understanding that manly discipline,
such a sweet hot guy, with such
a sweet hot body, and on the
college swimteam to boot!, how
i stood it standing there
outside his bedroom door,
me naked, it is dark,
i'm pretty sure he's not
asleep yet, i think
thoughts about crawling
into bed with him, but
i'm sure he's straight,
and i'm not actually
sure yet i'm gay, but
as i stand naked there
in the dark outside
his bedroom, everything
is real dark and real
quiet and the squirrel's
breath coming out of my
ears is making a slow
hissing sound, torrid,
lost,
stranded.

scooter

"i wonder what the squirrels are up to today?"
said the sexy big-dicked budding biologist high-school boy.
he said it kind of to himself, and kind of outloud,
as he stood in front of his bedroom window
and looked down at the ground.
three squirrels were chasing each other around out there.
"preliminaries to sex?" wondered the
sexy big-dicked budding biologist high-school boy.
his dick was hard.
he took off all his clothes.
the squirrels skittered about.
he tugged on his dick.
the squirrels ran half-way up a tree,
and then back down again.
he tugged on his dick.
the squirrels continued their scampering.
he grabbed a handful of kleenexes and
came.
he tossed the cum-soaked wad of kleenexes into the
trashcan, and stood there a while longer,
naked and big-dicked, in his room, staring
down at the frolicking squirrels.
"gee, they really seem to be having fun,"
the sexy big-dicked budding biologist high-school boy
said softly.
"is that the biological explanation to
everything?" he wondered. "is
everything about having fun?" he mused, outlining his
sexy little nipples with
just the tips of his long slender fingers.

greenpussysprouts

ralph woke up sweaty with
a hardon, speaking these words as
he awoke "he's
a mighty fine boy, oh he's a mighty
fine boy." ralph was
young and sexy himself.
and ralph had been dreaming
about X, a sweet
boy in his biology class.
yes, X was
definitely
"a mighty fine boy."
ralph didn't want to
be attracted to X in
this way, however.
in fact, ralph didn't
want to be attracted to
any boy, period.
yet, there ralph was,
lying on his back
with a hardon, thinking
about X.
**

ralph jerked off at
about warp speed, spurted
what felt like a quart
of cum, and then he
took a shower, and
headed off to school.
**

in biology class,
X sat down right beside
him. "guess what
i dreamed about last night?"
asked X. ralph's heart
was beating what
felt like a 100 miles

an hour. "what?" said
ralph. "i dreamed
that you and me
found a million
dollars in a sack in
the woods," said X.
"then we bought a
yacht with it," said X,
"and went off
fishing in the caribbean!"
"cool," said ralph.
then class started,
and everybody took
notes.
**

that night,
ralph woke up saying,
"he's
a mighty fine boy, oh he's
a mighty fine boy."
**

ralph had always
wanted a
yacht.

butterflies and sirloin

my one experience with being young has passed.
i had some fun while i was young, because i was young,
but i could have had more fun. but i didn't.
i'm getting old now, and am pretty pissed offed about
getting old, about my youth being over.
i just generally feel bitter and cranky.
mad at the ways things work.
people are born, live, and die.
some live longer than others.
some people only have a youth, and that's
it, nothing more. they die young.
me, i'm 58 now.
in my teens i was manic depressive and
i think that mental illness caused me to
miss out on a lot of potential fun.
in my twenties i was just a mess.
but i had some fun in my twenties, i'll
admit. sexy messy fun.
**

am i glad i'm still alive?
yes.
do i sometimes wish i was still 26?
yes.
do i often wish i still had the body
i had when i was 26?
oh yes.
**

it often seems to me, now, that
26 is the best age to be.
and yet i was a mess when i was 26.
didn't know nothin' about
nothin' except
how to have a great orgasm.
and there were a LOT of those.
a lot.
**

i drink a lot now, at 58.

i have a lot of great orgasms, too,
at 58.
yep, still...
let's be frank,
it's a whole lot more fun
to watch a sexy 26-year-old guy spurt cum
than it is to watch a flabby 58-yr-old guy
spurt cum.
there's no sense saying otherwise.
**
sometimes there's just no sense.

so how was your vacation?

the waves lapping the beach,
the feeling in the air was peaceful,
and suntan lotion, was everywhere, not
a spot of skin that wasn't shiny
with it, not a puff of air that
didn't smell of it, coconut oil,
tongues tingly, nostrils quivering,
full of sweet sweaty secrets.
one day a micro-brewery gave
away free samples.
they came to you.

lagomorphic medicine

the easter bunny was having pain upon swallowing, so
he erected a tent and moved in to get away from all
the stress. however, about 7 or 8 sexy teenage
boys started hanging out in his tent, whether
he was there or not, and they liked to smoke
grass and jerk off together. sometimes
they even jerked one another off, in varied
rhythmic manipulations of each other's big hard
cum-spurting teenage man meat. even though
the easter bunny was again feeling fine—
no more problems on swallowing— he
didn't move back home. he decided to just
live in the tent, permanently, and he accepted
the occasional presence of the 7 or 8
sexy teenage boys who hung out there from
time to time; sometimes they were
completely naked, and openly discussed
explicit sexual functionality without any apparent
embarrassment or inhibition. they enjoyed
watching the easter bunny paint all those
eggs, and, whenever, by accident, he
happened to break one, they immediately
dived right on in and consumed that egg.
they even learned the value of consuming
the shells, brittle bites, small pieces,
calcium good for what ails ya, be it
ear, nose, or throat.

experiencing any discomfort

the golden age has passed, leaving the
apple trees spent, and frayed.
where once there was miracle whip on
the kitchen table, there is now only
mottled, and fat-free, mustard.
gelatin burgers top the list of
on-site indulgences.
the drum that was once beaten with such
gusto, is now an end table, with an
old lamp on top, one that flickers.
the magazines on that end table
are barely read anymore. their
covers are ringed with the sweat-marks of
old drinks.
the aroma of freshly clipped toenails
remains a constant to be reckoned with.
and those who are looking for zero are
finding it readily available.
oh, yes, indeedee:
the golden age has passed, leaving the
apple trees spent, and frayed.

how many prawns can you eat?

the science of satiation says to keep on doing
something until you're full of it. teehee.
well, seriously now, the
science of satiation basically says,
you keep on eating until you
are full. then, you stop eating, because you
are full, and you don't want anything
else to eat, for a while anyway.
the science of satiation says to keep on doing
something until you are done, and
then you stop. for instance,
the beautiful big-dicked young man
keeps on masturbating, keeps on
rubbing and stroking and pumping away
on his big hard dick, until he
spurts cum. then, the
beautiful big-dicked young man stops
masturbating. and
the beautiful big-dicked young man doesn't
masturbate again until
he's in the mood again.
the science of satiation says the
beautiful big-dicked young man
will masturbate until he's done,
and then he won't masturbate anymore,
for a good while. but, that "good while"
part is open to interpretation.
the science of satiation is fuzzy on this point.
the science of satiation is indeterminant in
this area.
when does a person who has eaten
his or her fill need to eat again?
when does the beautiful big-dicked
young man need to masturbate again?
it is this "betweenness" in the
science of satiation that causes
so much head-scratching. between

one meal and the next. between
one masturbatory session and
the next. what does one DO with
all that betweenness? and, in
fact, how much betweenness
should there be? is there
some optimal amount of
betweenness? the science
of satiation is a world
of imprecision, of maybe's
and kinda's and sort-of's. when the
beautiful big-dicked young man
is masturbating, he is happy,
pleasant, and cheerful.
when the beautiful big-dicked
young man is eating, he
is happy, pleasant, and cheerful.
often, though, when he
is eating, he is thinking
about masturbating. when
will he get to masturbate again?
after dessert? or, should
he skip dessert, and get
right to the masturbating?
between meals, between
masturbation sessions,
drifting along in the
realm of betweenness,
the beautiful big-dicked young man
is lost, adrift, and
alone— as the scientists
of satiation congratulate
themselves on the knowledge
they've amassed so far, and slap each
other on the back, until
one of them says stop.

the patriot

as the fireworks
exploded in multi-hues up above,
one sexy young man was
so drunk that he stripped
off his clothes and danced
around naked, wagging his
big restless dick until
the cops took him away.
observers in the crowd
pretended to be appalled, and
dismayed, and outraged, but mostly,
they were more than entertained by what they
saw that night, as the fireworks
exploded, and the aroma of old-fashioned
apple butter imbued that
hot peppery gun-powder-scented air.

great expectations, marvelous

hydrogen lifted the big dirigible up into the air
and there it hung, just kind of drifting.
then lightning struck it, and the hydrogen
exploded, and the dirigible burst into flames,
and fell howling and groaning to the earth.
**

meanwhile, on the other side of the planet,
a sexy big-dicked naked boy stood kissing
his sexy big-dicked naked boyfriend.
their dicks were so hard and both of the
sexy naked boys were so excited,
that they both
spurted cum all over each other's
bellies, even though they
weren't quite ready for that to
happen yet.
**

the oranges sitting on a table
in a kitchen in vermont were
growing mold. it was blue.
it looked like blue frost
on the orange skins of
that bowl full of molding oranges.
**

somewhere in florida, a normally
gentle husband woke up from
his nap and fucked his wife
rather stridently, even though
she'd have rather not
been fucked at that particular
time in her life.
**

i mixed 25 drops of miracle-gro with
approx 1 quart of water yesterday, and watered
the ivy plant that's been
growing in our house
for over 10 years. it's

a beautiful ivy plant,
and i like it a lot.
i always water it with
miracle-gro and water.
it seems to love that
combo. its leaves are
dark green, and it grows
so fast, i have to trim
it frequently.
**

once upon a time,
i was 18 years old, and
i lived for 3 months
as a patient
in a mental hospital.
**

apples are never
actually really totally "red"–
that's something
you'll only find
in a paint store.

bow wow

you're thinking about getting a dog,
but now you're
in the middle of getting fucked by a
gorgeous ferociously big-dicked 18-yr-old boy.
the
gorgeous ferociously big-dicked 18-yr-old boy
is fucking you rhythmically and pleasurably
and he is sweating and you are sweating
and you are nearly beyond delirious in
your panting sexual ecstasy
and you are still thinking about getting a dog,
and the
gorgeous ferociously big-dicked 18-yr-old boy
is pumping away and
you're thinking what kind of dog
you might want
and the
gorgeous ferociously big-dicked 18-yr-old boy
keeps on fucking you and he's doing
A REALLY GREAT JOB!!, too,
god he is HOT! SO HOT!!
and you
both cum like
twin explosions
and then you say
"good boy!"
and then you say it even
louder:
"GOOD BOY! WHAT A GOOD BOY YOU ARE!!"
and the sexy sex machine 18-yr-old boy
says "arf?"

brillo pads

the swans floating on the lake are
dirty and gritty, their long necks
muted with grime.
the swans no longer seem to be able
to clean themselves, or each
other. they are not pure
and white anymore, but
grungy, soiled, dingy.
**
the sexy half-naked young man
standing on the banks
of the lake
watches the dirty swans,
and feels a tightness
in his chest.
last night he fucked
his girlfriend
for the very first time.
last night was
the first
time that he fucked
anyone, ever,
and yes, the
loss of his virginity
is a mystical
and oddly icky
presence inside
his tight pink brain.
**
the sexy half-naked young man
rubs his sexy little nipples
with his fingertips,
and watches the
dirty swans adrift
on the lake.
the smell in the
air is fungal,

of things forever
damp, a kind of
mildewy presence
in his flared-out
nostrils.
**

eventually the
sexy half-naked young man
stops staring at the dirty
swans, at their
long soiled necks, at
the oily-looking blotches
on their off-white backs,
and he heads on home,
to eat rice krispies,
and slurp up the
sugary milk.

water beans

water on top of a tin can of beans on the back
porch, a screened in porch— and there is
a film of water on top of that tin can because
it is raining, and the rain is blowing,
and there's so much rain that it is
sitting on top of that tin can of beans.
this tiny little microcosmic image
of the tin can of beans with water
on top sitting on the rainy screened-in
back porch
suddenly seems emblematic of the whole
entire world, the universe, everything,
to the shy skinny sexy young man who lives
in that house.
the shy skinny sexy young man
is standing in the doorway, looking
out onto the porch. he is looking
at that can of beans with the water
on top of it, that lightly bulging
meniscus of clear cold water that
bulges slightly upward, and
the rain continues, and
the air coming from that back
porch is cold, and what the
heck was he thinking, leaving
that can of beans sitting out
there for, anyway. perhaps
he'd planned to heat them up
in a pan on the cold metallic
barbecue grill, but that didn't
happen. so that can of beans
just sat there, and now it's
getting rained on, it and
the whole porch, cold, and
windy, and
the shy skinny sexy young man
begins to cry— he feels

embarrassed and pathetic,
actually, but he just stands
there and cries,
and wonders if it, life,
the universe, the world,
that can of beans, is
always going to be this way.
and, at that moment,
he's pretty sure
it is.

nests

the endowment which he had been given
was a great body, a sweet face, and a big dick.
he'd had to do no work at all to get all that.
it had just happened.
**

people liked being around him, too.
he was friendly, had a good voice,
enjoyed conversation– and being 23 years
old and lean, athletic, tall,
good-looking– all of that certainly
seemed to work to his advantage.
**

yet, he dreamed dark dreams,
his thoughts drifted down bleak and
despair-filled rivers; he often
woke in the middle of the night
and bawled like a baby, just
because he felt incredibly sad.
**

at times like this, if the weather
was good, he climbed out
of bed, put on shorts and tennis shoes, nothing
else, and went out running– sometimes
for miles and miles, through dark quiet
suburban streets in the middle of
the night. then, near the end of his
run, he ended up in the deep dark
middle of the municipal
golf course, where he
stripped off his shorts & shoes
and masturbated under the warm night
stars, spurting cum onto the
soft dewy grass.
**

if the weather was bad, he sat
naked in front of late-nite tv, whatever
was on, it didn't really seem to matter,

and he masturbated there;
he preferred masturbating in front
of something interesting on tv,
but he had found that even
the weather channel was satisfactory.
then, after spurting
a great deal of cum, he wiped
up, returned to bed, and slept
fitfully until the alarm clock rang,
at which point he got out of
bed, and again, uttered
his marriage vows to the world,
to the universe, to the stars and to
the galaxies
and to the vast expanse of vastness.
**

then, as usual, he floated
thru the day like a mote of dust,
greeting the other dust-lings,
cheating on the lunar debris.

specializing in art history

when the helicopter flew over,
rick's dick got hard, and
he anally raped his best friend jake.
they were in the middle
of a field of tall grass.
"ow ow ow" said jake.
"shut up and take it
you skinny sexy bastard"
said rick, as he shoved
his cock deep into
jake's tight pink asshole.
"ow" said jake. "ow!
goddamit! ow stop goddamn
you stop!"
but rick didn't stop
until he'd shot his
load deep into jake's
tight twitching asshole.
jake was down on his
belly, jake's left ear
was pushed into the ground.
jake's pants and underpants
were down around his
ankles. rick stood
up and looked down
at jake, lying
there on his belly.
rick pulled up his
own pants and pushed
his own big cock
back into
them and zipped
them up. "stand up"
rick said to jake.
"stand up and pull
up your pants."
jake stood up

and pulled up his
pants. he zipped
them, belted them.
then he turned around
and looked at rick.
it was a look full
of hate, and fear, and
nebulous misunderstanding.
"why'd you do that
to me?" said jake.
"just had the sudden
urge," said rick,
a sneer on his
handsome face.
"just had the urge,"
rick said again,
wistfully.
"well goddamn
you to hell,"
said jake.
the helicopter
flew over again,
this time lower,
and it was hovering
above rick and jake now.
anyone in the
helicopter could see
what was going on
down below. first
jake started crying.
then rick started
crying, too. they
were hugging each
other tight as the
helicopter hovered
and hovered and
hovered. the grass
was whipping all

around, and no one
knew what to do.

DNA

the smell of burning candle wax greeted his nostrils
as he walked into the old house, gently festooned
with holly wreathes and lit candles everywhere
he looked. he had been invited for a gathering
of friends. the owners of the house knew
he didn't get out much. the other guests
knew he didn't get out much. they liked him
anyway, because he was attractive, quiet,
and harmless. he never said anything
aggressive, offensive, or even the
slightest bit annoying. plus, he
was just so darn cute, sweet, good-looking,
and well, let's just say it: he was
sexy as heck, and nobody at all understood
his affinity for being alone so much, and
for politely shrugging off most advances
of friendship, socializing, or sexual adventure.
tonite, though, the hosts were pleased
when he walked into their home, as were
the other guests. he stood there
nervously smelling the burning candle wax;
it smelled good. he stood there
nervously looking at the holly wreathes,
which seemed to be literally everywhere.
oh it seemed like a very festive occasion, indeed;
and he chatted and made the smallest talk possible,
everyone looked him over, and he felt he
was being assessed for possible conquest.
he knew he was physically attractive. he
knew he inspired lustful sexual thoughts in those
around him. he stayed a while, had some
punch, cookies, endured some more small
talk. then he politely thanked his
hosts, and went out to his car.
he opened the door, climbed into his car,
and started it up. and then he
drove home, to the little one-bedroom apartment

where he lived alone. he'd painted
the walls with dabs of his own blood, and
blotches of his own cum spotted everything.
he took off all his clothes and ate
a can of tuna fish. then he went into
the bathroom and stuck a
q-tip way up his nose, until it bled.
he smeared some of the blood around
on the walls, and waited for his nose
to stop bleeding. then he
walked into his bedroom and jerked
off into a corner. he watched
his cum dribble down the seam
where the two walls met. then, once
more, he gave up and went to sleep.
his dreams were always so pretty, mostly
flowers and cotton candy, and pink, so pink,
always extremely, warmly, pink.

hero parsnips with succotash

the earth was once believed to
sit upon the back of a giant turtle; but,
when atlas came along to take over
that job, he quickly came into
favor because lots of people
just like to see a naked big-dicked
muscular guy lifting something heavy.
it accentuates stuff. ok?
but prominent displays by the pro-atlas
faction are still occasionally
encountered today, in the deep
dark woods, on moonlit nights,
when the taste of sweat on
the neck of your best friend
is nectar, wine, the best of the booze:
he offers you the entire sky,
stars and comets and everything,
but instead you compromise
and accept just the
planets–
cold, and distant, with
all their sad
little strings:
brittle, and
broken,
no hope of
repair.

black 'n' white checkered linoleum

the crunchiness of whole wheat toast between
his teeth was just dandy. he sat there skinny,
old, and wizened, crunching away on the
hot brittle crispiness of the just-slightly-
burned whole wheat toast, savoring its sound, and
remembering what being young was like: the
perpetual hardon, the smooth skin and
the general muscular tawniness of his aura.
he sat there in the kitchen
beside the toaster, crunching away,
thinking what it was like
to be young, everything made him
think about that these days, toast,
chewing toast, the
smug look on the face of the slowly melting
butter.

when it works

the music was loud and thrumming as the
two sexy naked young men sucked each other off.
each sexy naked young man writhed and contorted himself
with pleasurable ecstasy
and displayed tight sinewy muscle and hard thick dick
as he got sucked off by the
other sexy naked young man.
then, tangled all up together, their mouths fresh
with each other's semen,
they lay among the twisted and sweaty sheets and listened
as the loud music dwindled to sputter, and
then stopped.
"wanna pick another cd?" asked one of
the sexy naked young men.
"nah," said the other sexy naked young man,
"let's just lie here in the silence and
smell each other's armpits."
then both sexy naked young men began to giggle.
then they started laughing.
then they were laughing really really loud.
"i love you man," said one sexy naked young man.
"and i love you, too," said the other sexy
naked man.
and then they really did: lie there, smelling
each other's armpits, pushing their
noses in deep among the sweaty
curly hair, each sexy naked
young man getting more and more
turned on by the moment,
until it was all they could do to keep
from crawling down each other's hot slimy throats.

fluorescent mangos

nothing was obvious to him.
nothing was clear.
the smell of rainwater, so much like lavender.
the taste of whiskey, so much like happiness.
how could he be this good-looking on the
outside and feel this bad
on this inside?
it just didn't make sense.
in the heart of the forest, surrounded
by nothing but pretty things,
how could he feel as bad as he felt?
nothing made sense.
nothing followed logically from anything else.
sitting pretty and alone in his spiffy apartment
surrounded by nothing but pretty things,
it would seem he should feel, well,
better, wouldn't one think it would
work out that way?
that wispy beard he was growing,
was starting to seem like a good idea.
he didn't know why, exactly.
but he decided to just let it grow.
might as well. meat on the
table, meat on his bones. where
was the logic? perhaps in the marrow;
there in the long calcium tubes
slimed with oil and
bits of salty red pepper.

a while ago

lose count, and the skunks of your past
will trample down your door,
exude their foulness,
and drink the tepid water from
your fish tanks. then,
still not satisfied,
they'll demand an episode
of *I Love Lucy* on
your DVD player, with a side dish
of mustard-pretzels.
then, and only then, will they
leave, but you just know
they're not done with you yet.
every little sound: the
possibility of
skunk footfalls, black-and-
white fur musty
and dirty between their
obtuse little long-nailed
toes.

equals

wild men often have a few good years, then burn
out like a flare.
and who's to say the goal should be longevity?
who's to say that quantity trumps quality?
maybe the wild men only ever wanted a few good
years, and that was enough for them.
everything else was just a bother, nothing
to be looked forward to.
yep, a few good years, and then
well, if not death, then
something like it.
just drifting in a haze,
coping with what's left.
those few good years, though, wow!
wild men wouldn't trade 'em for anything.
not even a signet ring with superman embedded
in the clear lacquered stone.

ceremony

the solemnity of the occasion was marred
only by the secret joy among sequestered members.
oh, everybody was polite, deferent, and
respectful, but, you just knew what
some of them were really thinking.
**

after, there were sandwiches, chicken legs,
and potato salad.
**

much later, there was booze, a lot of it, too.
most of the sincere frowned on the booze,
but they didn't have to know about it.
**

MUCH later, there was secret secret sex.
picture two tall lanky attractive naked young
men, sitting on the couch in front of
a pornographic movie, jerking one another off.
after, they sat there with cum all over
their sweet sexy tiny-nippled chests,
giggling, drunk, warm, and happy.
**

i mean, it's not like anybody had a
monopoly on answers, or even suggestions.
**

and, after a while, there
was a very nice sunrise, pink, with, like,
purple streaks of fibre
scrambled all through it. stunning,
really. almost mitochondrial, but not
quite that wet.

weenies

migratory patterns of gregarious creatures amaze
and befuddle. ducks, geese, starlings,
grackles. monarch butterflies.
blankets of life, settling
onto fields, or floating on ponds,
or coating the branches and twigs
and bark of
well-placed trees. or hiding there,
resting, on their way, near-invisibility
achieved by green-feathered warblers and
ruby-throated hummingbirds.
biological miracles.
phenomenal zoological events.
gnus and water buffalo, traveling
toward water, rain, life.
people at the beach in july.
does that count?

vernal

at the strawberry ball, all the catering is
done by college swim-team boys. they all
walk around in speedos only,
showing obvious obtuseness, mounds
of strawberries on their bright shiny silver trays.
whipped cream for dipping dots the spectacle.
the air is filled with the scent of
ripe strawberries. guests are awash
in the miasma of the atmosphere; there
is an aura of olfactory and gustatory
delight. miniscule digressions from
proper behavior are rare, but
generally involve fingertips placed
on items other than strawberries
dipped in whipped cream. there's
a swimming pool in the center,
filled with warmed fresh spring water,
no chlorine added, no chemical scents,
just a layer of strawberries floating
on the surface of the water. the
layer of strawberries is 3 or 4 inches deep,
deeper than that in places, and
the surface of the water is red and polka-dotted
with a zillion strawberry seeds, with
bits of green leaf poking out here
and there. occasionally
a swim-team boy dives right on
in, leaving his tray on the floor
beside the pool, his mound of
strawberries greatly diminished,
barely a dollop of whipped cream
to be found. once safely in
the pool, and underneath the
layer of strawberries, he's quite
invisible: still though, everyone
knows he is there.

a bit of whimsy for the susceptible proofilites

strike up the band.
roll out the barrel.
there's a weedy blither blather of wit-smarfs
holding court. there are tall ones,
short ones, fat ones, thin ones.
there are green ones, white ones,
pink ones, yellow ones, crayon-colored
ones.
it's quite a mix.
they all talk earnestly. some speak
of death. some speak of forgetting
the past and moving on with the
jelly bean eating contest. there is
quite a bit of discussion on that
issue until the cute sexy naked
young men show up and begin
publicly masturbating. these
young men have big dicks, too. real
big. there
is spectacting. there is lactating.
there is near-hemorrhaging, but not
really. what a summer day it
becomes as the butterflies land
freely on the heads of whomever
they choose. some think it's
the sign of god. some think
it's the sign of the devil. there
is much more discussion than
usual. meanwhile, the sexy
young men have all spurted
their daily allotment of cum
and walked away, far out of
sight. even though they
are out of view, there is speculation
that those sexy young men are
touching each other in inappropriate
ways. there's a flurry. hot wet blizzards

materialize and roll over plant
life. it's a real miasma of
matriculosity. there's farting.
burping. gnashing of toothy knees.
you want conflagration, those folks
will show you how to conflagrate. these
wit-smarfs eat well, and often.
but there's no real appreciation
of their food. they don't live
like that. it's better to say
that in the month of june, they
prefer july. nobody asks real
questions anymore. everybody's
too sure of everything. oh how
the little dogs laugh and kiss
butt. all mules (be they male or
be they female) are normally sterile, but
they fuck anyway and sometimes
all their fucking pays
off. have you ever heard of a
baby mule that had a mommy mule for
its mommy instead of the normal
configuration which is a daddy jackass
and a mommy horse? no? thought not.
well that's because
mules are hybrids (jackass x horse: two
different species) and most
hybrids are sterile. but every now
and then, there's a fertile act
of copulation mule-wise-speaking,
and then you wind up with a pregnant mule
grazing in your pasture and
if all goes ok you've soon got a
cute little baby mule on your hands.
maybe you'll
name it "blue moon" because it's
that rare. now wit-smarfs just love
getting their hands on one of those rare little

"blue moons" and making it one of their own.
they pet it till
it thinks it's loved. in reality,
though, the washboard copyright
of the inactive session is more
than anyone can fathom, and
the jelly bean eating contest thank god
goes off without so much as
an ecstatic quiver. all
the little "blue moons" of
the world are just bone-dry sterile; actually it's
in fact the law. they're cute though.
but sexy naked young big-dicked masturbating men
spurting
cum, that's pretty cute too.
now now none of that.
no not a bit; they mean business, baby,
those wit-smarfs, oh
how they mean business plain-speaking pointy-pouts
that they dearly are.

the pangs of separation

spatial relationships befuddled him.
for instance:
put two people in a room, and how close are they together?
when he saw a picture of a triangle on a page,
and tried to turn the image of that triangle upside down in
his mind,
what did that image then look like?
streets wound mysteriously throughout the region, the
towns, the cities, coalescing into various intersections
that gave access to a variety of dwellings or businesses
that suddenly seemed to appear, as if out of nowhere,
as if out of a dense smarmy fog.
oh yes, to this spatially-confused young man,
sexy, skinny, and wild-eyed, the way things fit
together with other things would remain
an eternal mystery. the only thing that
made any sense was the throb of his own orgasm,
the smell of another man's cum,
platefuls of boiled shrimp and brightly
colored spicy vegetables.
everything else was a mish-mash of jumbles.
and so, he lay there naked sexy and sexed-up
beside the man he loved: how close could
two people get in the same room? and
when the space between them approached
zero, what was the shape of all that
other space around them? subtract
the two of them from that space,
and what was left, that volume
that he and the other man had
occupied, suddenly available,
as it were, for intrusion.

brushwork

and so all the leaves changed color and fall arrived.
walking in the woods became a multi-colored
near-psychedelic dream.
for a shy sensitive sexy slender sexed-up young man,
it was a wonderland for masturbatory indulgence.
he walked there daily, after school, amongst
the foliage, amongst the craggy tree trunks,
crackly insects making their strange crackling sounds,
lizards skittering here and there, birds
near ultra-loud with the intensity of their
autumnal squawkings and murmurings.
the shy sensitive sexy slender sexed-up young man
took it all in, as he walked naked and
wide-eyed and wild-eyed and his big smooth
satiny dick fully erect as he walked there
amongst it all, there in the forest,
the colors vibrant, the smells of mossiness
and approaching decay. he paused often
and gave himself over fully to his masturbatory
desires, standing there in the woods
pumping on his big smooth penis,
his pink nipples sweaty and tingling,
anointing the leafy mossy moldy ground
with puddles of cum, there in the
land of techno-color and the tension
of the approaching winter lapping at
his toes, smelling his tight pink little asshole.
shy sensitive sexy slender sexed-up young man
walked on, smiling sweetly, the look
in his eyes, goofy, and wise, and wild.
there were a few droplets of shot cum
that clung to the tops of his toes,
and the rest of it dried there behind,
where he'd marked his territory like
a dog that spurted cum instead
of pee. he did it all quietly, except for the occasional
yelp of joy, there in the multi-hued forest,
before the certainty of winter.

radishes are red, too

the sexy big-dicked teenage boy is thinking about martians
while he is jerking off. the sexy big-dicked teenage boy
is lying naked on his broad well-muscled back and
tugging on his big smooth dick while thinking about
mars and the martians, martians who, at this very moment,
may be roaming in armed bands over that planet,
gathering provisions to load onto their
ships and carry those provisions to earth
as peace offerings and/or weapons, whichever
may be deemed appropriate. and as the
sexy big-dicked teenage boy lies there naked
in his bedroom jerking off,
he envisions the martians taking off from
the planet mars in their big smooth shiny
ships and heading toward the earth, intent
on war or peace, it doesn't seem to matter
to them, just as long as they arrive
here on the surface of our rich ripe
planet, and as the sexy big-dicked teenage boy
lies there naked on his back pumping away
on his cock, he envisions the little naked
footprints the martians are
making as they step onto the desert soil of nevada,
the plowed fields of iowa, the dusty playgrounds
of seattle, and the sexy big-dicked teenage boy
starts spurting big hot gobs of gooey cum
that spatter his chest and belly and
dribble into his wiry lightly-musk-scented
pubic hair, and he lies there spurting
cum thinking about the martians, longing
for the martians, so hungry for martians
that his mouth waters and spit trickles
down his cleft and handsome chin.
"gotta love them martians," he whispers,
and then he giggles so charmingly, it's almost
like he's not alone.

again

milk in the refrigerator makes a dandy place
to rest your hand on a hot day.
put your hand on the milk-filled carton
and just stand there.
think about stuff for a little while.
then close the refrigerator door
and walk around in the kitchen.
moan, if you feel like it.
you know the drill.

ozone

ballsy guys will say darn near anything
to darn near anyone.
ballsy guys get a lot of
action in the bedroom.
ballsy guys are
dream-tickets to the
bridges of passion, heart-breakers
from way-back, used
to disappointing folks,
accustomed to the sweet
smell of success. sometimes,
a ballsy guy and a mousey
guy will get together, and be best friends.
a ballsy guy and a mousey guy together,
the ballsy guy plows right on ahead,
and the mousey guy gets to follow along,
share in the spoils of innumerable
victories. there's little conflict;
there's never any doubt who's
in charge. the ballsy guy
asserts; the mousey guy
hangs around for laughs.
when life throws a mean twist,
though, the ballsy guy
and the mousey guy have
been known to get a little
too comfortable together,
in their efforts to comfort
one another. they always
stop short of having sex
with each other, though.
almost always, anyway.
a rainy night a few weeks after
a death in the family, the
aura of gloom is palpable,
life seems senseless,
and the ballsy guy and

the mousey guy are
sharing their secrets;
lightning flashes
and, well, things happen,
there on the couch
in the half-light
of love.

sore

when transplanting seedlings, the sexy
young-man works in the nude,
out behind the greenhouse,
among the shards of broken flower pots,
his naked toes amongst the old silt of sifted peat moss.
sexy young-man working in the nude
carefully transplants the small seedlings
into the next-stage pots, bits of
fertile soil on his chest and nipples
and spilling into his navel and pubic
hair and darkening the tip of his
smooth pink cock-head– he works
and works and transplants and
transplants out there behind the
greenhouse. when he gets thirsty,
he stops and takes a drink out
of the nozzle of the slinky green
hose. then he squirts himself
off and washes away all the clinging
bits of soil, and he stands there
wet, shiny, and
the whole thing– the complete
image, everything, him, the
seedlings, the sifted peat moss snuggled
at his toes, his broad smooth
sweaty back, the nozzle
of that big green hose pressed
to his lips, his freshly-washed
but previously soil-darkened
cock-head– it's all so
sexy that the ornaments surrounding
the fish pond,
statues of big-busted mermaids
and goat-footed fawns,
wriggle, flex, and
ask him for favors;
he never says no.

they only really want
a good scrubbing– so much
moss and algae clinging
to their perpetually
wet surfaces,
but he always gives
them more than that.
never complains, either.
never. well,
maybe every now and then,
when he's feeling
cranky, sad, and
just plain
lost

a life in whispers

during his speedo-wearing phase he looked marvelous
and fell in love with listerine: he used
it morning, noon, and night.
**

he swam literally thousands of laps;
won medals, ribbons, and trophies.
**

his love affair with listerine was well-known,
and generally well-tolerated.
**

he tried to make a few bucks out of it, but
the folks at listerine didn't seem all
that interested.
**

later, as his looks began to fade and things began
to sag, he decided that speedos were
completely and utterly out of the question
in terms of self-attire;
he turned to running laps instead of
swimming, and he ran in sweat pants
and sweat shirts— he didn't look bad, either—
just, well, not as good as he used
to look.
**

soon
he started seeing dust where there was none.
he started thinking maybe dust was
bits and pieces of those who were dead and gone,
but who were not completely gone—
**

lingering, as it were, like
tired footfalls, mildewy
swimsuits, the occasional crinkled & gray pubic hair
clinging
like taxidermy.

nocturnal bio boy vs. the algebraic blues

in the high-school showerroom,
the two naked boys Sean
is talking with are very attractive,
but Sean seems to be unaware of that.
**
Sean himself is naked, too. Sean
is attractive, too. they are all three
talking about the algebra
test that they will all be taking
that afternoon.
**
Sean likes biology a lot more than he
likes algebra: he likes all those bio words,
and all those bio ideals.
**
Sean & the two other good-looking
naked boys talking
in the shower surrounded by
other good-looking naked boys– this
image appeals to Sean as
he gradually starts to see it
as though he is viewing it from
several feet above, and silently, too.
**
at the end of the day, in his own
little bedroom, after the
algebra test, after he's done all of his
homework, Sean falls asleep. Sean's dreams
are mostly about
naked boys, and when
he wakes up in the middle
of the night,
the quadratic formula reeks
of insensitivity, smells like
irrelevance, water lilies the milk of all foliage, the
essence of all those highly sought and tiger-eyed clams.
**

yes it's
tempest time in the
sheets of biomorphism:
mathematically it's bleaksville, and
big-time biology trumps everything yet again.

review

the magenta green nature of the ice
on the smooth slick pond
belied the true nature of
what was being covered up:
the body that floated beneath
in a kind of cold-induced lullaby:
naked, male, young, pink.
it was shocking, really,
the calm tranquility of his
expression under that smooth
slick ice. when he opened
up his eyes and pushed his
fist through the covering,
shattering it, banishing
the tranquility, and climbed
out onto the surface shivering
and shaking like a big blonde
dog, easily 6 feet from
top of head to sole of foot,
it was apparent
that the approval level
of the audience went way up,
and the geiger counter readings
shot through the roof. after
all that, the triumph
of the naked, the ascension of the young
and the eerily sexily beautiful–
it's what they all wanted, really,
deep down inside their dark little
barely-beating hearts.

pissing on potted plants

when you're insane, is everything you do insane?
or just some of the stuff.
getting up in the morning and putting on your clothes.
is that insane? what if you get up in the morning
and put on your clothes when all you really feel
like doing is dying and you don't REALLY care if you get out
of bed or not, but you just do it, out of habit?
running laps.
what if you're insane and you're running laps?
pretty ordinary. probably not an insane act.
brushing your teeth.
what if you brush your teeth so hard your
gums bleed and then you keep on brushing and
brushing and brushing and watching the
blood drip from your mouth and still
you keep on brushing? harder and harder. and
harder.
when you're insane, is everything you do insane?
walking to work.
what if it's only 4 blocks to where you work?
not too insane to walk the 4 blocks.
what if it's 4 miles?
well... what if it's 10 miles? and you
walk to work? and it's pouring rain.
hmmmmm.
so this guy is totally insane, diagnosed
and the whole bit, and
he makes the most beautiful watercolor
pictures you could imagine, and today
they sell for big money. yet this
same guy used to swallow anything
he could get down his throat, including
bits of pens and pencils broken into
sharp jagged pieces.
since he was insane, was everything
he did insane?
how about going into the store and

buying the tubes of watercolors
and calmly paying and walking out?
and then going home and before
he got down to work
he went out on the beach
and stripped naked and swam
in the water and then
climbed out and lay down
on the beach where he masturbated for
about an hour
and then he got down to working
on his watercolors.
if you're insane, is everything
you do insane?
dining by candlelight in
a fancy restaurant with a friend, drinking
lots of wine, banishing the ache
for a while.
just a while, though,
just a while.

different

squid ink on the tabletops.
squid ink on the sheets.
squid ink on the showerroom walls.
yes, for some reason unknown to medical science,
the sexy big-dicked teenage boy
spurted cum that looked like squid ink.
black and oily.
even just a tiny bit gritty.
embarrassed, the sexy big-dicked teenage boy
had gone to the doctor for examination.
after several tests,
the doctor had declared both
the sexy big-dicked teenage boy
and the sexy big-dicked teenage boy's
cum
"normal." "with just an atypical pigmentation."
"nothing to worry about."
still, though,
the sexy big-dicked teenage boy felt odd,
and strange.
he knew from pictures in dirty books,
and from pictures on computer screens,
and from the testaments of his friends,
that human male cum
was just not supposed to look like squid ink.
one afternoon, jerking off with
several of his cute male friends,
everyone just kept talking about
that "squid-ink" cum of his.
comparisons to each other's
cum were inevitable.
his was the only cum that looked like that.
there were smirks and chuckles.
at night,
the sexy big-dicked teenage boy
often dreamed of life underneath
the sea. in his dreams,

far below the ocean waves,
he sprouted tentacles, and,
when danger threatened, he
hid himself in clouds of squid-ink cum.
in the morning,
his sheets looked like a Jackson Pollock
painting,
or a Motherwell oil,
free and wild and uninhibited– exactly the
same emotions that
he wished
he felt, but didn't.
squid ink on the tabletops.
squid ink on the sheets.
squid ink on the showerroom walls.
it was all just kind of creepy.

lawrence

the miracle of boredom is that it sometimes
begets creativity.
and masturbation.
and, on really good days, creative masturbation.
for instance, today the sexy big-dicked teenage boy
stirs himself from his boredom and
strips himself naked and paints his
nipples red with a tube of red lipstick.
then, what the heck, he paints his
scrotum red, too,
with the same tube of lipstick.
**

the house is empty. he is all alone.
**

so there he stands, in front of
his big bedroom mirror, totally naked,
his nipples painted red,
his scrotum painted
red, his big dick hard and
smooth and throbbing.
then he jerks off with
a few fast well-paced pumps of
his fist, and
it's off to the
shower with him, where
he discovers it takes LOTS
of soap and water to
remove lipstick.
information that
may prove useful
some day, he supposes.
**

he hums a while
in the shower,
a new tune, one
that he's just now
made up.

can't hear you

behind the waterfall is mist and loud.
people have slipped off and died back there.
people have crashed into the stream
while bouncing around on the rocks
as they fell. legends are rampant
of ghosts of this cute naked
boy, ghosts of that cute naked
girl, haunting the place, the
mist, the falls that go
crashing down onto rocks and then
into the stream. it is sure
loud back there behind the
falls. it is especially
dangerous back there now,
in winter, with all that
ice all over everything,
as two sexy young men,
in search of excitement
and total solitude,
stand there in the iciness
behind the falls and kiss
each other on the lips.
furthermore, they have unzipped
the zippers of the each
other's trousers, and
are fondling each other's
big smooth exposed cocks as the
falls flow over the two of them,
the two sexy young men with
their hands all over each other's
dicks, the falls are
loud and misty, ice
everywhere, the two
sexy young men kiss
each other on the lips
and fondle each other's
big smooth cocks, and,

when the two sexy
young men spurt cum,
they sigh and smile
and suck on each other's
tongues, the sexy ghosts
of sexy dead boys and
sexy dead girls,
hover for a moment,
as if remembering.

pop goes the weasel

for him, the sexual side-effects
of viewing carnage were
undeniable, and he always REALLY enjoyed
sexual activities after a good
horror movie– a horror movie that
had included lots of
blood and gore. he was tall, skinny,
had a nice face, a big smooth dick,
and a sexual appetite that was
definitely whetted by the
viewing of a nice dollop of
wet messy horror-movie carnage.
in fact, he'd experienced some of the best
orgasms of his life right after
viewing a blood-soaked carnage fest.
in fact, he'd experienced some of
these orgasms WHILE viewing
a blood-soaked carnage fest.
there was this one time, sitting
in the front seat of his
car with his girlfriend
at a drive-in movie, that
during the most intensely
bloody portion of the movie,
he had guided his girlfriend's
hand onto his massive throbbing
hardon, and the handjob she
gave him resulted in, well,
he still remembered the explosiveness
of the event. lucky he had
a spare shirt in the back seat; the
one he was wearing was soaked
with his own cum. oh that smell.
that car seat. her hand
on his massive throbbing
cock during that one decapitation
scene... sometimes he wondered

if there was something wrong
with him. ah well. what the fuck.

undomesticated

THIS PLACE IS HAUNTED thinks the
beautiful big-dicked boy, his
big dick as hard as a shiny steel pipe.
chains are rattling in the background.
there are moans and sighs. a big
dog, more like a wolf, really,
stands shivering in the middle of
the room, blinks,
squints, then trots off into
nothingness. THIS PLACE IS
FUCKING HAUNTED! thinks the
beautiful big-dicked boy. he is
standing naked in the middle
of a big smooth room. there
is a large rumpled bed, and a few
over-stuffed chairs. the light
is dim. he doesn't know
how he got here, why he's
here, how long he's been
here, but his big hot dick
is hard and throbbing, and shiny
like steel, in the strange
phosphorescence of the light,
whose source he is unable
to discern. the room is
just strangely glowing. he
himself is shiny like
metal– beautiful and big-dicked
and horny as hell as chains
rattle, voices moan and groan
all around him, and the big
dog, yes, it is a wolf! no
doubt about it, the wolf
returns, growls, then
breaks into sobs and moans
that sound very much human.
the beautiful big-dicked

boy walks over to the wolf,
pats it on the head, and
the wolf's eyes turn white-hot,
and sugared cherries fall out
of its open mouth. the
beautiful big-dicked boy
bends down and eats,
starving for food,
and company.

phantoms

quite the large number of crows gathered
there at the edge of the
cornfield, there where it
meets the fence by the stream
that runs along the
property line where
the teenage boys come
to smoke and drink
and take off
their shirts and
talk about sex.
no teenage boys yet,
though, today– just
the large number of crows
gathered there,
as if waiting to
be forced off this
spot by the arrival
of the young, the
smooth, the wild-eyed,
the trash-talking,
the smoking drinking
shirtless swaggering. the
crows today mill
around on the ground,
picking at this and
that; cigarette butts
appear to catch the
interest of the crows,
as do discarded
cigarette wrappers.
what do crows build
their nests with
anyway? buttons
popped from collars,
thread still clinging.
bits of this, scraps of

that, cigarette
wrappers plastic
and crackling and
shiny like new moist
lips.

at the molecular level

the smell of metal on a cold day
is terrifying. in a train yard,
for example,
all that cold metal, tracks,
trains, parts of trains,
steel bolts, sliver-angled iron shafts
holding the tracks to the
icy ground. terrifying. awful.
to be trapped there for
even a few moments, the
warmth being sucked right out
of your body and into
all that cold flat gray metal.
terrifying.
you can smell the near-frozen grease.
**

in a sculpture garden on
a cold day– all those
statues of naked men
and naked women in
vibrant active poses; they
look like they should be
warm, but they're not– they're
cold, icy, same temperature
as the coldness that surrounds
them, perhaps even colder,
and you, alone in
that sculpture garden
on a cold cold day.
you can smell the frosty bronze.
**

makes you long for
heat– perhaps you think
of hot sexy naked young
men on hot sandy beaches
under the blazing sun,
lying there in the

sand, their arms and
legs wrapped around each
other, there on the hot
sandy beach under the
blazing sun.
you can smell the tanginess of
slippery suntan lotion on tawny,
shiny, pheromonally-charged young skin.
**

in the train yard, in
the sculpture garden,
on the beach, on hot days,
on hot days when
metal radiates
heat instead of sucking it up,
things go on there,
in the summer, on hot
days, coins strewn haphazardly on
the hot sand, flesh and cigarettes
and booze, the dead cold
a banished thought, an
unspoken word, a fear
that foments revolution.
you can smell the smoke.

14-hour drive

as i recall, "mouth breeders" refers
to a group of fish that carry their
eggs, and babies, in their mouths to protect
them. but if you think i'm going
to "look it up" now, all these
years later, when i don't have
to take another goddamn biology course
ever ever again, ya got another
thought comin'.
**
yep, i took a lot of biology
courses. that's what i majored in.
i knew a lot of facts about
biology. still do, actually.
even though i'm 55 years old,
and all those biology courses
were a lonnnnng time ago.
**
once, in a genetics class, i
spotted the handsomest guy
in the world– blond, tanned,
stunning blue eyes– and
ended up figuring how to
talk with him, and we became
friends. he even took me
to meet his parents in
their house in Pensacola, Florida.
**
i always refer to him as
"Pensacola Steve" now– he
got married years ago– haven't seen
him in forever.
**
when i took a shower with
him in the dorm, his body
was astounding; just wonderful;
compact, but not too compact,

with lots of muscles. nice
dick, too– adequate, but
nothing too flashy. jeez,
he was a nice guy.
**

met him in a genetics class.
just one of all those biology
courses i took.
the genetics professor was
6' 10" tall. certain things
one remembers; a mouth breeder,
carrying all those babies
in his mouth– it was always
the males that did that part
of the job; some things one
remembers; some things one forgets.
**

white Pensacola beach sand clinging
to Steve's nipples; the sand so
white and the glare so strong,
i couldn't focus on anything but the
nipples.

tendon

"me me me me i'm just
so me-centered. when will
it ever stop? when will
i ever really care
about anyone or
anything else?" thinks
the sexy record-breaking
collegiate swimmer,
as he stands up from
the toilet, flushes it,
and adjusts his speedo
to perfect ball-hugging
cock-defining fit,
and off he strides
toward the pool
and satisfaction
and victory,
the flex of his
own muscles the glide
of his own skin through
the blue-tinted
chlorinated water
will leave him
giddy almost sick
with joy, high
as a white fluffy cloud,
serious masturbation
to follow soon
thereafter, and then,
as usual,
when he's spurting cum
he'll be thinking about
the possibility of
finding his long-lost twin,
a constant fixation of
his: the find, the two of them,
him and his identical twin,

together: it wouldn't
really be incest,
not really, DNA being
what it is, and
flesh moody as a
dream.

vergil died 19 B.C.– and scott's pecs

the truth is,
the sexy naked big-dicked teenage boy
has the hots for scott, president
of the high-school latin club. scott is
a bodybuilder. scott has
won teenage bodybuilding competitions
locally and nationally.
scott is a high-school senior.
the sexy naked big-dicked teenage boy
is a high-school junior, and he
has the hots for scott.
his
having the hots for scott is
a secret, though.
truth is,
it's quite doubtful that scott is gay,
and
the sexy naked big-dicked teenage boy
doesn't admit that he, himself, is gay.
but there sits
the sexy naked big-dicked teenage boy,
alone on his bed, his latin iii textbook open
on his desk, his
vergil assignment
awaiting translation,
his big thick dick hard and throbbing,
and he's thinking about
vergil, and latin,
but mostly he's thinking
about
scott.
soon, the sexy naked big-dicked teenage boy
just lies back on his bed and starts
jerking off: for a few blissful
moments, his mind seems clear,
precisely focused, on the
wonderful feeling that his own

highly stimulated great big hard dick
is giving to him.
as he spurts cum, he pictures
scott's broad sexy bodybuilder shoulders,
the open page of that latin iii textbook,
and vergil's voice sloshes
around inside his head
like doom gone wild,
death a certainty,
where is vergil's body today
anyway? probably just
dust now, and
the sexy naked big-dicked teenage boy,
his chest and belly drenched in his
own cum, rotates the image
of scott clockwise, counterclockwise,
and the years spin by like
latin— everyone spoke it
back then— even
while getting fucked.

degree

out of the slurry of the coal fire, strides
the hottest boy you could ever imagine.
he looks to be about 18 years old,
but who knows? maybe
he's really 500 years old, or 5000 years
old. who can tell? but he strode right
out of that fire,
naked, sexy-looking as all get-out,
hair on fire, his eyes shy,
and yet eager, too.
try to touch him, though,
and your hand gets
burned. try to kiss him,
and you'll pull back
before you feel the sizzle.
he's naked all the time.
no need to try
to put clothes on him, though,
they'd just catch
fire and burn off anyway.
he likes to sit in the
local coffee shop, and,
if anybody's coffee
gets cold, he just
grabs ahold of the cup
for a couple seconds, and
that heats it right back up.
he seems to appreciate
the thank-you's that
he receives. they seem
heart-felt, and genuine.
he likes that, being
appreciated for something
he can do rather than
for what he looks like, as
he sits at the corner
booth, the one with

the metal chairs,
their sharp little
feet melting the
wax on the
cold slick floor.

wrestling with change

when the percolator malfunctioned, coffee
went all over the kitchen:
the walls, the countertops, the floor.
well, the two sexy young men
had been in the bedroom
having sex during the percolator malfunction.
when they walked naked and
sweaty into the kitchen and saw the
mess, one of the two sexy naked young men
said "FUCK!" and the other of
the two sexy naked young men
said "GODDAMNIT TO GODDAMN HELL!"
**

clean-up took a long time,
and, during the process,
the two sexy young men
threw the old-fashioned
percolator out into the back yard,
and left it lying there,
like a little gray corpse.
**

then they went out and bought
a brand-new drip-style coffee maker.
they had liked that old-fashioned
percolator, though. it made
good, rich, old-fashioned coffee.
the new drip-style coffee maker
wasn't bad, though, they
had to admit, that evening.
they stood there in the kitchen,
and stared at the new gadget.
"it does look pretty good,
doesn't it?" said one
of the two young men.
"yeah, kind of like a space-age
rocket launcher doesn't it?" said
the other young man.
**

then they went into the den,
watched an old movie on tv,
and, when there was a part
in the movie where an
old-fashioned coffee percolator
was making coffee,
the two young men smiled
wistfully.
"damn percolator," said one of
the two young men.
"but i do kinda feel sorry for
it," said
the other young man,
"lying out in the back yard like that,
all cold and alone."
**

in the morning
they gave it a decent burial,
near a rose bush,
a red one, with
especially big thorns.

shopping list, folded in the middle

time standing like a dinosaur
poised to pounce,
as the sexy big-dicked country boy
sucked on mark's big schlongy
hard pumping dick.
the sexy big-dicked country boy
and
his cousin mark
only did this the one time,
and then it was over,
a thing of the past,
never talked about ever
ever again between them,
or to anyone else,
as far
as
the sexy big-dicked country boy
knew.
now,
the wind moving the willow leaves
and their long feral branches,
the sexy big-dicked country boy
is a man, with wrinkles
on his face,
and memories inside
his warm moist brain
that skitter and spark from
brain-ridge to
brain-ridge, and
fire like pistons, as
if still having the
very best time of their
little wet pink lives.

early winter

the bones in the school yard are mine.
they are what is left of me.
human bones.
my bones.
i know this makes no sense.
very little does. that's the
trouble with expecting stuff
to make sense when it doesn't.
have you ever watched a sexy big-dicked
teenage boy jerk off and then
watched him spurt his cum?
he just knows it feels good,
what he is doing. it doesn't
need to make sense that it
feels good. it just needs
to feel good. that's all
the "making sense" that is required.
perhaps this sexy big-dicked teenage boy
wants to stop masturbating, feels like
he does it too much. but he can't stop.
because it just feels too good
to give up.
one day he'll be a pile of
bones in the bottom of a box.
or a scattered pick-up sticks
of bones lying around in a school yard,
with a few vultures hovering
around, perhaps
hoping for a few scraps of flesh
that might still be clinging.
hope is a funny thing.
you can't really explain it, other
than sometimes when you want
things to turn out a certain way,
they sometimes do, and that
gets you to have expectations
for the future. good expectations.

good expectations for the future.
that ain't a bad definition of hope.
listen, my bones are bleaching
snow-white in that school yard,
while a sexy naked big-dicked teenage boy
spurts cum. he wishes things
could always be this way:
cum-spurting and cum-spurting
and cum-spurting, world without
end. but there are
clouds on the horizon,
funny twisty things
that go bump in the night,
squirrels that eat brains
instead of
peanuts.
or should that be the other
way around? as a matter of fact,
maybe everything should be
flipped over,
and tasted for authenticity.
lord knows,
a few good olives,
can make a good day
even better.

twist and shout

the muscles at the back of his neck
were so sexy they were practically like
his genitalia. i watched him
drying off from his shower.
my roommate. a swimmer on
the college swim team.
a sweet sexy guy.
we were both 19.
we were both good-looking,
him better than me, but
still, both.
now, at the age of 58,
looking back, and
back, i understand
that i was gay,
and wanted to be
straight. and that,
nonetheless,
i was in love
with him:
college swim team
swimmer with a great
body and wonderful
smile
and that, he,
no doubt, was straight.
there was nothing
he could do about
being so sexy,
though, nothing
he could do about
my secret lust
for him.
sometimes stuff
happened. like
when we went camping
together, we rolled

together for warmth
on cold winter nights,
the snow pelting the
outside of the tent,
us huddled together
for comfort,
and warmth, our
voices low and
soft, seduction
could have been
in the air,
sex pumping
heart pumping
his voice deep
my voice not
as deep, together,
our two voices,
a gently throaty
rumble as
the snow fell
and fell
and fell.

slide over

on his back, beside the dumpster,
he inhaled bad smells,
and watched the sky.
he was drunk,
just turned 21, abandoned
by his so-called friends.
it was night, maybe
1 or 2 am,
and there was a full
moon, and that was
all the light he
could see in the sky.
he was sexy skinny big-dicked
and tall. and, oddly enough,
he was naked.
how this happened, he
was not quite sure,
but he was pretty
sure his so-called
friends had stripped him
and left him like this,
lying drunk beside
this smelly dumpster.
he stood up,
wobbled,
felt his dick
wagging free and
loose in the cool
evening air.
this was awkward.
he heard giggling.
he heard some more giggling.
then, his "friends"
walked out from behind
some bushes. one of
them was carrying a bundle
of clothes. "did ya

happen to lose something?"
he heard. there was
more giggling.
his head was fuzzy.
the moon was really
bright, and, he felt
really weird, but he
laughed along, just
like everyone expected,
and, for once,
things didn't turn out
too damn bad. in fact,
after they'd dressed him,
he was soon
back in his own little
apartment. then
everyone went away
except for mark, his
favorite of the bunch.
he was in bed with
mark now, they
were both naked,
and mark
smelled really really
good, like spring-time
mint leaves,
but even
better.

sherwin-williams

in some parts of the country, it's
a homeowner's tradition: everything in
the yard (except
the grass itself) gets painted white:
every rock, every birdbath, every
busty concrete mermaid statue,
even the lower 3.5 feet
of every tree trunk– all painted white.
**
at night, there's kind of an eerie
glow from all that white paint.
**
at night, there's
just the hint that maybe the
practice of painting everything
in the yard white is kind
of charming and weirdly nice, like
the people who do all that painting
know what the heck it is they are doing.
those yards do look kind of inviting
now don't they...
**
in fact,
**
sometimes,
sexy teenage boys escape from
their bedrooms and
naked smoke and drink
beside white rocks and
lower 3.5 feet of white tree trunks.
sometimes these sexy
naked teenage boys get smoke-drunk
and erotic-happy and
jerk off together, out there
in some unsuspecting yard,
amongst all the white
objects: then,

all done,
wander nocturnal neighborhoods
on tiptoe, on delicate hoof, among
the white rocks;
only the
dribbles give them away.

enter at your own risk

the spell was cast over the empty parking lot
as he stood peeing beside his car.
toads on the outskirts of the pavement
were twittering and clicking and clacking,
making all kinds of eerie amphibian sounds
as he stood peeing beside his car.
the pavement was hot, and his pee
splatted, almost hissed, and splashed
onto his tennis shoes while he peed
and listened to the little toads
in the distance.
he was sad and lonely, sexy and 17, his
big dick hanging out meaty and substantial
as he peed alone in the parking
lot, in the middle of that hot summer
night. after he'd done,
he pushed his dick back into
his pants, zipped up,
and got back into his car.
he started the engine,
but didn't put the car into
DRIVE. sad and lonely, sexy and 17,
he just sat there and listened
to the sound of the engine.
his thoughts were spinning around
kind of mish-mash inside
his head, and there was
nothing in particular he wanted to do.
so he just sat there
and listened to the sound
of his car engine,
the parking lot pavement hot,
and the night all around.
he listened to the sound
of the engine, strong
and dependable:
there was nothing else to do, so

that's pretty much just what he did
until the big cop drove over
and asked him to move on along,
so then that's just what he did,
the windows open, and him
breathing in the
steamy night air, swallowing
it as if it were
nourishment, tasty as
beer breath on the lips
of the one that he'd thought
he had loved.

growth rings

when it came to botany and
the gentle sexy big-dicked boy,
pear-shaped poinsettias perplexed him,
the nature of their curves,
the soft protuberance of their tips.
christmas and pear-shaped poinsettias
just didn't seem to go together.
who'd invented this mutant poinsettia
anyway? and why had it caught on?
**

opening his presents,
the gentle sexy big-dicked boy
discovered a big bag of marshmallows,
and reverted to his primal state
of howling tumescence;
his dick wasn't exactly
leaking cum, but it wasn't
really spurting out, either.
just a sort of spotty discharge.
**

poinsettia sap is milky white,
and poisonous. if you get it
in a cut, the cut will
burn. so try not to
break either poinsettia leaves
or flowers, because their white
sap will leak out and
potentially hurt you, especially
if you've got a cut or scrape.
don't rub it in your eyes, either.
jeeez, show some common sense.
**

the gentle sexy big-dicked boy
enjoyed the texture of the
marshmallows, as he chewed
whole-heartedly and endorsed
the smear of sugar on his

big pink tongue. the cat
knocked over the
pear-shaped poinsettia and
spilled it, and the soil,
onto the floor.
clean-up was slow and
laborious, but,
at least by the end of
the job, that
damn poinsettia was out
of the house.
**

roasting marshmallows at
the fireplace is a family
pastime that will long
be remembered. just ask
the gentle sexy big-dicked boy,
and he'll tell you
it was just like a dream.
a bright slimy one,
with red droopy flowers.
**

when
the gentle sexy big-dicked boy
grew up,
his own children
played wild in the forest,
and everything they brought home to him,
was a gift from the
heart.

all quiet

the georgian tectonics of the speedo situation
resulted
in lots of sexy naked young men
dipping their dicks in watercolors and then
drawing watercolor pictures of themselves, naked,
hungry, eager for companionship, but,
alas, alone, alone, alone.
**

the dawning of advanced civilization
required
self-understanding, conceptualization
of the meaning
of midnight waking up hot and horny
and eager
for cum-spurting. certainty was sought,
a surcease of sorrow,
but mostly
sexy naked young men who wake up
horny in the middle of the night
just do
what sexy naked young men
have done for centuries:
they tug on their own big hard smooth
dicks until they spurt cum all
alone naked on their backs
in their lonely beds,
or,
they go to the beds of
their fellow sexy naked young
man friends, and, together,
they spurt their cum,
speaking in parables and hyperboles,
of sense and sensibility,
of
puberty vs maturity,
excitement vs the mundane,
as the clock

strikes 1 a.m., and the
stars twinkle like madness
gone public,
the reefers of desire
the plains
of
reason.

the sensation of really thick breadmold

the error in the belief system of post-scriptum thinking
means that ravioli on the stovetop sometimes
boils more than it should, while little birds
in the backyard are chirping like magnets,
and three sexy naked big-dicked teenage boys
hidden away in the bedroom
are sucking on each other's big thick cum-spurting dicks,
and the yellow in the teacup is camomile, the
gentlest of all the stomach calmers.
**

there be dragons in the
land of mist and rain,
where little does the meaning of
trilobite flute-playing
impart to the interactions of
daily persimmons on their
way to market.
**

actually, persimmons are rarely
eaten anymore these days– a shame,
really. a real darn shame.
**

after a hard frost,
persimmons are soft and mushy,
their flavor sort of pumpkinny,
as october grabs the
scarecrow, and shakes it
half to death.

90% clean

this morning on my way to work i saw a sexy
mostly-naked young man who was running through
wisps of fog. he wore only a paper-flimsy pair
of shorts and a pair of tennis shoes. he
was tall
and tan with dark hair. his
shorts were black. it was quite
early, and
as he ran mostly-naked
along the side of the road,
running in fact off into
the grass,
i strained to take in every
last bit of him, every
last detail, before
losing sight of him
in my rear-view mirror
and heading toward
my parking spot
in the near-empty
parking lot, thinking
how beautiful he was,
how long a day is
ahead of me,
how even now,
he might be taking
a shower after his
early-morning run,
might be soaping his
big sturdy dick,
tugging gently on
his big sturdy
dick right before he spurts
his early-morning cum,
everything on schedule,
everything so goddamn orderly,
everything so goddamn

precise.
**

it also occurs to me now that
i didn't actually see his shoes,
tho i assumed they were there.
was he actually running barefoot,
are his toenails smooth and neat,
or ragged and jagged, like a pink pair of
claws.

what if

specifically,
the green of the car wash,
the lurch of the drunken man.
these kinds of things are meaningless
unless you love the car wash,
unless you love the drunken man.
**
i once rode through a car wash
whose soft green liquid glow was so
exotic that i still remember it.
i once loved a drunken man
who never drank.
he was just drunk on life
all the fuckin' time.
i'd have fucked him in an
instant, though it never came
to that. though we did
take lots of long hot
showers together,
in the college dorm,
a magical environment where
darn near anything could have
happened,
like in the car wash,
when
the green glow of happiness
could have
stained the
skin
of the strongest man,
made little boys
weep
with giddy bubbly
excess.

pragmatically speaking, guava jellies stain

the flight of the albatross takes us to the
land where girls in short skirts hunger
for the touch of sexy big-dicked boys.
nights on the beach are torrid secrets
of pendulums that swing in the breeze
as the first grass skirts fall from
the slender waists of sexy big-dicked boys
and the boy-hungry short-skirted girls
manipulate their own curious set
of soft-textured textiles.
soon, it is dawn, and
the albatross drifts on,
over open water,
and drags its toenails across
just the very tips of the waves,
the sunlight on the
water the most delicate shade
of lavender,
as the boys recount their own
adventures of the night before,
the girls touch their tender
nipples
where once forgotten
battleships dropped their
anchors
and lusty
sailors vied for each other's
attention.

a job

i was once a lab technician
in a college of
veterinary medicine.
i don't do that for a living anymore
thank god
yet occasionally i can still picture a big
dead bloated horse on the necropsy
table, it is an old dead stallion, and
as part of the procedure, we are
cutting off its big dead genitalia
and sticking them in a formalin-filled bucket
for something or other, some kind of examination
by someone or other, i forget who i forget why
i'm sure there was a good reason, several good reasons,
to examine dead stallion genitals.
also i worked
in the bone museum.
all the bones were carefully labeled
with little tiny painted catalog numbers and all
the bones were kept precisely
in their proper places so that they could
be readily retrieved for study
by students of veterinary medicine.
everywhere i sat, everywhere i stood,
something important was going on.
belly-shaved dogs, freezers filled
with frozen cow stomachs.
knowledge whirled around me
like bad smells,
i could smell it through the charcoal mask stretched
wet and soggy and tight across my face,
knowledge: people wanted it, were bent on getting it,
there were days i swear even the
flies sucked it up like
fresh blood, flew around buzzing like fat
furry thirsty little demons who would
never get enough.
well. i did.

beans

reeking of fresh semen,
he walks into the room
and waits to be noticed.
the semen is his own, splattered onto his own naked
chest during a hot
masturbation session only 10 minutes
earlier and then left
there under his t-shirt, which is
now damp and blotchy with the oozy gooeyness
of his own sticky cum.
he who wears the scent of his own
semen is young– a college
sophomore as a matter of fact– and he is tall, sexy, blonde,
lanky, hot-looking; he has great lips. he wears tight
faded blue jeans. and that semen-dampened t-shirt. the
t-shirt is white, with a black-and-red image of Mickey
Mouse on the front, cum oozing gently around Mickey's ears.
the room into which he walks
is a large room, with
about 3 dozen young men in it. any one of these
young men he can tell at a glance
he would be willing
to do intimate sexual things with. there is not
an ugly young man in this room.
he has never worn his own semen as cologne before.
today he's done it as a lark. and because he
feels, well, sort of evil. sort of angry.
sort of "in-your-face." sort of pissed off
at the world. (sort of, to use an old-fashioned
expression, "full of beans.")
the room into which he, reeking of cum, has just
walked, is in a private home,
the home of a professor of english literature.
it is a big, old, Georgian-style house, and,
the only UGLY man in this particular room is, in fact, the
professor of english literature. the long-time
partner of the english literature professor is

a sometimes perky/sometimes-pouty little man, also
ugly, but he is out of the
room at the moment, fetching ice.
the 3 dozen ATTRACTIVE young men are all students
belonging to the gay and lesbian campus group.
today's occasion is an afternoon party for this group,
to discuss books, politics, ideas, & ideals.
this time, only gay young men have
come to the party. no women have attended.
there is rumor of a schism. there is a rumor
that the women are forming their own
separate group. which is just fine with
he who wears the semen-scented t-shirt. (frankly,
he'd much rather look at boys.)
the ugly english literature professor
is talking to 3 or 4 attractive young men now.
they look bored, but polite.
he who carries the heavy musk of semen-scentedness on
his chest walks up to an
attractive young man at the opposite end of the
room. this attractive young man is wearing long pants,
white, and the shape of his big smooth cockhead is
clearly visible against the fabric of those white
pants.
"hi," says semen-shirt boy.
"hey," says cute white-pants boy, wrinkling up his nose
in a surprised and thoroughly interested manner.
"wanna fuck me outside in the garden right now?" says
semen-shirt boy. he says it loudly.
"er, um, er, um," says cute white-pants boy.
ugly english literature professor has wandered over.
"and you are???" ugly english literature professor
says to semen-shirt boy.
"i am trying to get fucked by this cute boy," says
semen-shirt boy. "we want to use your garden. we'll
find a secluded place. one with lots of bushes. we
promise."
"um, er, uh, um," says cute white-pants boy.

"i'm afraid this is not that kind of gathering," says
ugly english literature professor, trying
to smile through the look of horror and disapproval
that has captured his rictic face. and he seems to
have detected the odor of fresh semen, and is
eyeing the moist Mickey Mouse face of semen-shirt boy's
white front-dampened t-shirt.
by this time, semen-shirt boy has taken the hand of
cute white-pants boy and has started to
lead cute white-pants boy out of the big old elegant room.
"nevermind your goddamn garden," says semen-shirt boy.
"we will
go fuck our brains out in the big dark forest that is
miles & miles away. i have my car."
semen-shirt boy says these words loudly, as he pulls cute
white-pants boy toward the door. cute white-pants boy does
not have to be pulled toward the door with very much
effort. cute white-pants boy
seems both aroused and amused by the direct language
and non-subtle approach of semen-shirt boy.
ugly little partner of ugly english literature
professor enters the room carrying a little glass bowl
of melting ice cubes.
ugly little partner gives semen-shirt boy and cute
white-pants boy the eye.
"not leaving so soon i hope?" say ugly little partner
of the ugly english literature professor.
"afraid we must," says semen-shirt boy.
"um er uh, ummm," says cute white-pants boy.
and with that, semen-shirt boy and cute white-pants boy are
out the door, in semen-shirt boy's car, the windows
down, the car going at a fast speed toward the forest,
toward sex, toward wild and hedonistic abandon, an
afternoon of unbridled sexual passion and
multi-orgasmic pleasure. it's a little later now,
after they have parked the car and wandered into
the forest.
"i like it much better out here than at that

stuffy old party," says semen-shirt boy to
cute white-pants boy. only now,
neither boy is wearing any of those items of apparel.
in fact, now, neither boy is wearing any apparel at all.
birds sing. breezes rush through the leaves and pine
needles of the trees that loom overhead. "and god i hate
english literature," says semen-shirtless boy, as he
lies on his back, on a bed of moss, his legs lifted and spread
wide, with his toes almost touching his
broad sexy shoulders.
cute white-pantsless boy pushes his big smooth
cock deeper into the tight pink asshole of semen-shirtless
boy. "ummmmmm, nice," says
semen-shirtless boy. "and,
as a matter of fact," adds semen-shirtless boy,
"i HATE literature. period. i HATE the word. i HATE the
term. it all just sounds so goddamn PRISSY, doesn't
it?"
"um," says cute white-pantsless boy, "um um um".
"exactly," says semen-shirtless boy, "now fuck me faster, ok?"
cute white-pantsless boy obliges, thrusting more quickly
than before, and even more deeply.
"ummmmmm" says semen-shirtless boy. "you're good. you're
hot. you're goddamn huge, too."
cute white-pantsless boy slobbers now; the slobber drips onto
semen-shirtless boy's smooth sexy chest. it mixes
there with the dried semen, and, as he's getting
fucked,
semen-shirtless boy rubs the slobber into his skin
with his finger-tips, and smiles really quite
maniacally. "ahhhhhhh" say the two boys. "ahhhhhhh."

bipolar stadium

the mitochondrial smear of gloom essence
hangs in the air like
duck-billed platypuses on their backs,
exposing their enigmatic genitalia
to the peregrinations of the wind.
**

it is a bally-hoo pom-pom-toss kind
of day. cheerleaders exude, well,
let's just call it "extreme
enthusiasm" shall we? rampant insistence on the
unity of effort and theme
pummells the heads
of the spectators, 99.9% of
whom are really "into it."
the others
aren't so sure.
**

athlete uniforms are tight,
and certainly accent the phallic, &
the scrotal.
**

up above, big clouds billow,
threatening rain. in fact,
if one squints, one can
see the millions of raindrops,
preparing to launch themselves
earthward, toward the crowd.
**

birds dart in and out among
the blackness, eating
quick-flying insects, or hoping for sex.
**

when the rain begins,
no one goes home.

whimpersville

magruder the cute filling station attendent;
he's got big hands, too, with long fingers.
**

makeshift the way to his heart; grease
the pathway to his well-lubricated emotion.
**

settle on down for the long haul; get your
gasoline there everytime you have to fill up.
**

sure gas prices are rising, but it's well worth it
to be able to see him, those eyes, that voice, deep,
rumbling, innocent, knowledgeable, all of that,
everything about him. you fill your own
tank, though. if you got him to do it,
he'd lose all respect for you; besides,
you'd hate to seem too obvious.
**

the filling station where he works at is at
the top of a long smooth ridge in the highway.
lots of business; it's a car repair place, too.
you don't want him to work on your own car
though. you take it to the dealer instead.
you like lots of things about getting
your gasoline there at the filling station
where he works at, but, when it comes
to touching the insides of your car,
its deep inner parts and places, well, reason
must prevail, sensation of the head
must realize above sensation of the heart.
**

his name is jason; his big smooth
cock bulges lazily against the front
of his striped greasy coveralls; sometimes
he mans the cash register, takes
money from your fingers; yes, he's
a jack of all trades, master
of everything he touches, or so it

seems to you: the voice
in that throat of his; the exquisitely short
fingernails, almost brutally maintained;
brevity of contact. that's the key
to this engine, baby, the starter switch
to a day in the sunshine by the clear
glistening lake; oil-sheen on the surface but a
prelude to deep warm wetness at the toes.

my money's on the t-shirt he keeps under the front seat

the testosterone trucks, pickups, with one two three or
four men inside,
zoom by in the mornings on my way to work.
i picture all these men as
sex-hungry studs. i picture them going home to
their wives or girl friends after work, and just fucking those
women
non-stop; and, on top of that, the women really really like it.
they yip and squeak and writhe as those big-dicked men
slide and glide and pump and push and shove their
big dicks into
the vaginae of the their juicy sex-loving women. it goes on
half the night, the women yelping, the men pumping,
the men spurting near an entire pint of cum into their
women before the night is done. then the morning arrives,
they fuck their women one more time to do something
about their regular clockwork-dependable morning-hardons,
the sex-loving women moan and groan and cum as their
big-dicked men moan and groan and cum, and then
those men are outa there,
on the road, in their pickup trucks, driving mean, or
riding mean, zooming in and out of traffic, on their way
to work.
they don't seem calmed by their night of fucking. they
seem charged, energized, electrified, post-fuck mean.
i picture their big thick dicks still hard against
the insides of their stiff pants. i picture
them sitting there in the cabs unabashed showing
hardon and not another one of the men in the
cabs even takes a peek. they all sit there swearing
and work-thoughts-directed and thinking of the fucking
they did last night and the fucking they'll do tonight,
and those testosterone-filled pickups zoom between
cars and between 18-wheelers, zoom toward work and
muscle-flexing
muscle-taxing mechanical electric chores. sometimes
i do wonder about the pickup trucks that contain only

a driver, and nobody else. those trucks move pretty
mean, too. i can almost never see the driver's face,
but it generally looks hard, stern; sometimes the driver
is kinda young, cute, sexy. but the eyes are cold.
i think he's thinking of his well-fucked girlfriend;
she was well-fucked last night, and she'll be well-fucked
tonight. his dick is hard. he's alone in the truck.
one hand is on the wheel. i'm pretty sure where
the other hand is. maybe: his pants are unzipped
entirely, his big cock jutting out of them, and with
that
free hand he is jerking himself off. zooming in and
out of traffic, one hand on the wheel, the other
hand on his big cock; he moves skillfully along
negotiating all obstacles. i wonder where the
cum goes when he spurts it. and i'm sure he
spurts it; he couldn't just sit there stroking his dick
thinking of the fucking he's done and the fucking
he's about to do, and then not spurt— just
zip it back up hard into his pants. nah, he spurts all right.
but into what? and where does it go. ah, the mysteries
of the road, the wonders of the highway.

squid fuckers

the big-dicked sexy naked boys killed
the squid by fucking it to death.
it made odd rubbery gurgling
sounds while they were
fucking it. they made slits
in its big gray body with
knives, and then they
inserted their dicks
into the slits, and fucked
away. the squid didn't
bleed, not conventionally
anyway. it kind of oozed
grayish-green-yellow slippery
fluids, which made a sensual
lubricant for their big dicks
as these boys jammed their
hardened ramrod-stiff dicks into
the holes they'd made in
the squid flesh. a few times,
before it died, the squid
did seem to be in pain.
its flesh kind of quivered
as though an electric charge
were sizzling through it,
and a couple of big tentacles
flailed about helplessly. one
or two of them grazed the
naked backs and butts of
three or four of the hot
sexy sexually-frenzied boys
who were fucking it, but
mainly, it just lay there
and took it, a big squid,
too, its being-fucked body
at least 30 feet long, not even
counting the near-languid
tentacles; the number of boys

was 14 or so, all
fucking away at once,
slobber draining from their
open mouths, watching the
squid die, watching their
peers fuck with wild and
near-angry youthful frenzy,
the big gray body of
the dying squid. after it
was dead, after the last
boy had spurted the last
of his big gooey wads
of cum into it,
the sexy big-dicked
broad-shouldered, ripple-
bellied boys stood around
naked staring at it.
then they waded into
the water, washed the
strange squid juices
off of their dicks
and bellies and hands
and feet. in fact, they
pretty much submerged
and just rinsed around
out there in the water,
the blazing sun beating
down on their broad shoulders
and wide backs and hair-plastered
heads and faces as
they popped up
out of the water
and exchanged looks that were boyishly
quizzical, even slightly naive and
goofy— and yet there was an edge,
too, to the looks they gave each
other. the looks they
exchanged were

confident, cocky
as it were;
there was a sense of pride,
there was a sense of accomplishment:
there was a sense that
they'd gotten away with it
this time,
and, that, next time, by golly,
they'd get away with it
again.

suddenly! grabbed by nostalgia!

when i was in college,
i lived in the dorm, and
it hurt real bad falling
in love with my roommate, a straight
guy who was on the swimteam, and
was who was very very sexy.
and it was all kinda complicated.
for instance, back then i hadn't
really admitted to myself
that i was gay. in fact, back then,
i pretty much thought i was straight.
i didn't think i was in love with him.
i just thought i liked him a lot.
i didn't think i wanted to suck on the
big purple-pink perfectly-shaped cockhead of his
big smooth athlete cock and have him squirt
his hot gooey cum directly into my mouth.
i just thought i
liked him a lot. and, in fact, he
liked me a lot. in fact everything
he did in regards to me
was utterly warm and totally friendly–
and because he was so nice and fun
to be around and on top of that a real-live
honest-to-gosh actual hunky
athlete, i found myself in the position of
being liked by, and liking,
a really sexy nice warm
friendly athletic young man. in short,
he was precisely the
man of my dreams. though of course i would
never have phrased it that way then. we did
all kinds of stuff together:
tennis, swimming, backpacking,
eating dinner together every night.
eating breakfast together every
morning. we showered together a

lot, actually. we showered together
in the big gymnasium showerroom after
we worked out in the gym. and often we
showered together there in the big
dorm showerroom that was down
the hall from our room— just because we liked to
talk while we showered. sometimes, to be honest,
we took 2 or 3 showers every day, depending
on what kinds of activities had immediately preceded.
tennis, for instance: after we played
tennis together, we always
required a shower, and we
took it together. or after going out for a run together,
we required a shower, and we
took it together. hot sweaty college boys,
always getting oily and sweaty and needing
to wash it all off,
that was us!
and we liked to clown around in the
shower, too; for instance, by cupping his
hands just so, he could squirt a stream of ice
cold water 10 feet with perfect
accuracy onto my dick when i was
shampooing my hair and my eyes
were closed. we could talk about
anything. oh yes, i was
in love with him all right.
no doubt about that now. he was
kinda the center of my whole entire life
there for a while.
we lived together in the dorm, and after
that, we lived together in an apartment,
and after that, we lived together in
a great big double-wide trailer
on top of a hill with a view of
the mountains & other trailers.
there in our trailer, sometimes
he stood naked in the bathroom & talked

131

with me while waiting for me to get out of
the shower. we didn't actually
shower together in the little bathtub in
either the apartment or in the trailer.
i remember it was kind of an adjustment,
actually, when
we first moved out of the dorm and into an apartment,
having just a regular bathroom
with a regular bathtub and a regular shower.
we had grown used to big showerrooms with
lots of showerheads to choose from and lots
of room to move around. but
it seems we accommodated to the situation of
having just a normal bathroom by talking naked
in that bathroom a lot, actually. it sounds
kinda gay now, i know, but mainly i thought
it was just because he was so gregarious he
liked company all the time– and he liked
my company a lot, which was nice, and yet
torture because of course even though i
was still trying to be straight, i
thought he was real darn sexy and i loved
him. the sight of him naked standing in
the bathtub nearly took my breath away.
he dated lots of girls. and sometimes
he did sexy stuff with them. i know.
sometimes i could hear them in
the next room. i dated girls, too.
but i didn't do the sexy stuff as
much as he did. i know that for a fact.
standing there in our bathroom in our
trailer, me drying off naked, and him
naked getting in a few more comments before
jumping into the shower himself,
it's difficult to fathom that
i really truly didn't know that what i wanted most
was to be touching him every place on his
gorgeous sexy swimteam athlete

body that my fingers would reach, with
special emphasis on his big smooth dick and
his great-looking tight little ass.
later, after college, we stayed
in touch for a while. but then
when i finally figured out i
was gay and started seeing
another guy– this one gay, thank
goodness!– and told my sexy athlete former
roommate that i was gay and seeing
somebody, well things just
kinda fell apart between us. no
big scene, really. he sent
me an envelope full of christian
propaganda– i think that
was something he'd found
after we graduated. he was
sure never the christian-go-to-
church type of guy while we were roommates.
anyhow, after that envelope, that was
pretty much the end of it. we never
saw each other again. but here i am
now, thinking about him, for whatever
reason. i guess it's just true: sometimes
nostalgia really DOES just sneak up and grab ya! and
i can picture him now quite vividly:
he was a sexy guy that
i loved, would probably have
had sex with if the opportunity
had ever happened, and who
disappeared from my life. his smile
was infectious. his sense
of humor was fantastic. he was
smart. he was an athlete. he was
just totally, totally HOT.
for a while there,
he made me feel really really good,
and yet it's also undeniable that he

made me ache in ways
that approximated pure and painful
torture. that cock. those lips.
that wet pink tongue. those tiny little
swimmer nipples. i wonder if actually they
were all as off-limits to me
then as i was sure they were at the
time... i wonder...
anyhow.
that was my college roommate.
and that's who i fell in love with,
all those years ago.

too beautiful

the night color of the grass,
the snot-covered sheen of the moon,
the smear of his own cum on the
sexy young man's bare naked chest,
this is the total image of
sexy naked young man sneaking
off to the back yard in the middle
of night and stripping off his
shorts and t-shirt and lying
there naked on the grass under
the night-time sky, stroking
his big thick long cock
until he spurts his cum
onto his chest and lies there
staring up into the vastness;
it seems an unlikely place
for him to start shedding
tears, but it's not the
only place he's ever cried.

pure pleasure, thematic musings, beautiful male flesh

when the wildebeests are upon the land
and the lure of pumpkin batter is inescapable,
there will be gnashings of teeth.
there will be spikings of hair.
blue tri-tone will rule.
beautiful young men will strip themselves
naked and stand in front of their mirrors,
agonizing. is touching a body this
beautiful, even if it's your own
body, a homosexul act? is watching yourself touch
a body this beautiful, even
if it's your own body, a homosexual act?
thoughts occur, subside, rouse.
and then they stand there naked and
big-dicked in front of their mirrors
and watch themselves masturbate, watch
themselves stroke their big smooth
purple-headed dicks, watch
themselves spurt pints of hot smelly cum that
dribble down the cold glossy surfaces
of the mirrors.
as their knees go weak and buckle from
the multi-jib-jab sparks of too much pleasure,
there's a hint of doubt that anything
that feels this good must be
trouble.
naked sexy big-dicked young men
put on their clothes and go out
roaming the planet,
licks lipped wet with their own
spit, eyelashes batting
helplessly in the face of
bitter desire. milkweed plants grow
tall and furry and release their
white puffy seeds into the breezes
that underscore the horizon.
at dusk, tears are shed, and

it is assumed that if anybody
notices, they'll pretend not
to, or say something brilliant,
or at least, something.

sardines

oh what a wild and wanton wind that blows its way
into the mucky wanderings of the young and
high-spirited. it takes them by surprise,
rips off their clothes, touches their genitalia,
presses their lips tightly against their own teeth.
it tousles hair, tangles it, wraps and unwraps
it, assembles strands in savage and unkempt ways.
the young writhe in its path, welcome it at
first, then, they're just not so sure what
to do, what to expect of this rough fondling
they are receiving from it. their naked skins
glisten tawny and tingling, their fingertips
when lifted above feel as though they
could leave their fingers, fly off into
the sky, print themselves on the butts of
birds. there is a constant moan and drone
as of dishes under watery assault in
the dishwasher. eventually, the young and
naked just lie down on their backs
on the ground, staring up above,
the wind whooshing over their nipples
and over their thighs and fanning
their pubic hair as though it were
wheat about to be
flattened in the fields, and, then,
it is over. suddenly, the wind
has stopped. the day is nearly
done, and there they all are
lying naked on the ground like that,
skin tingling, and everyone's feeling
a little silly now, but, their
eyes are glowing, and the taste
on the tips of their tongues
is salivary delight, and
the thoughts are of ice cream,
and cup cakes, and other things, too—
things you're not supposed to put
in your mouth.

first love

besides
Roy Rogers on tv when i was 6 (and that
doesn't really count)
it was a
high-school
basketball player
tall + skinny
with a deep
gentle voice
we were lab partners
in advanced biology
we dissected a fetal pig together
+ a huge dull-green grasshopper too
i never said
or did anything
to let him know
i'd have slept with him
in an instant
an all-night camping
trip would've been
perfect   but
this would of course
have meant that
our relationship
went deeper than
a dead fetal pig
+ a big dead grasshopper
i peeled back skin +
muscles   imagined his
zipper his underpants parting instead
labs were odd affairs
his long thin legs folded
beneath the table he'd try to keep
them out of the way
yet sometimes one of his
knees would bang the
underside of the table

+ lift it annoyingly
he always apologized
+ his apologies
were sincere
it's just that
his legs were so long
at night my wet dreams
reeked of
formalin and
sweaty basketball shoes
i chewed grasshopper legs
+ wept for dead baby pigs.

next to the rope burn

i have smelled the motor oil on his breath, and
i liked it, the desecration of the spaniels,
the array of meaty sandwiches on the kitchen cabinet.
tall and tanky, with greasy armpits,
vile manners and despicable customization
standards, he scrapes the old paint
off the barn, and slops on the new.
trawling for secrets in the depths
of the ocean, he brings back
giants, and squid ink, and
bags of flesh-wet shells, their
siphons poking out in desperation.
i offer him coffee, but he
demands whiskey. the fate for
displeasing him is
hardcore sex. the fate for pleasing him
is more hardcore sex.
there is the smell of rockymountain
goat dung in the tight air
of our living quarters.
when i brush away the dog hair,
he insinuates bactine.

twice the size of our regular brand

millipedes on the resplendent landscapes of
theoretical principles of sex and sexuality
fascinated everyone, of course,
but none more than the
sexy naked big-dicked teenage boy.
when he thought about everything,
about the hair and the aroma and
the slipperiness of it all,
the millipede on the
stepping stone in the backyard
rolling up into a ball as a way
to protect itself from harm,
the sexy naked big-dicked teenage boy
knelt down and studied the
creature, the spiral of the
coil, the legs tugged in tight,
its little head protected in
the very center of the coil,
golly what a pretty creature
it is,
and
as
the sexy naked big-dicked teenage boy
stares at the millipede which has
rolled itself into a coil on
the stepping stone in his
backyard,
he contemplates being out here
naked,
hoping no one will observe
him out here,
where he shouldn't be naked–
it's not like he's an exhibitionist
or something, it's not like
he wants everyone to
see his big throbbing dick,
a part of nature as

sure as
the yellow dragonflies,
currently laying their eggs
in the crystal-clear fishpond
that his father loves
like a son.

working through it

two sexy young men, one who is depressed,
and one who isn't, standing
in the depressed guy's apartment, late at night, talking,
just the two of them:
the depressed guy says: "i have seen your dick and i like it,"
and then he gets this weird crazy kind of expression
on his face, as if he's asking himself
NOW WHY DID I SAY THAT?

the guy who isn't depressed says: "i can get undressed if you like."

the depressed guy says: "i don't know."
the guy who isn't depressed says: "let's just both get undressed
and cuddle on your bed. i bet you'll feel better."

the depressed guy says: "i'm not in the mood to have sex."
the guy who isn't depressed says: "you say that NOW."

the guy who isn't depressed smiles charmingly, and his
eyes flash signals of aliveness and zest for life.

the depressed guy has tears welling up in his eyes.
the depressed guy feels really really morose.

the depressed guy says: "i'm really not planning on
having sex, ok?"
the guy who isn't depressed says: "hey! you
know me after all this time, i hope! no pressure!! but let's
just get undressed and cuddle. sometimes when you're
feeling down like this, it helps just to lie
there with somebody you like. and i hope i'm still someone you
like???"
the depressed guy says: "of course you are."
the guy who isn't depressed says: "that's good."
then,
the guy who isn't depressed adds, "and you're
someone i happen to like very very much, ok?"

the depressed guy nods, kind of listlessly.

the guy who isn't depressed takes off all of his
clothes and stands there in the living room
of the depressed guy's apartment.
the guy who isn't depressed is hot-looking, naked,
sexy, sweet face, beautiful lips, big smooth cock.

then, the guy who isn't depressed says, "OK now!
let's see that sexy sexy body of yours!"

but, so far, the depressed guy has only taken off his
shirt. the depressed guy looks good that way– shirtless–
he is lean, has muscles, a byronic face, with dark sad eyes.
the depressed guy stands there shirtless in his own living
room looking lost, confused, ill-at-ease.

the guy who isn't depressed says: "oh come on now,
off with those shoes, young man! and off with those
pants!" he says these
words very cheerfully, encouragingly, gently,
with a twinkle in each of his mischievous eyes.

the depressed guy sits down on the couch and
starts unlacing his shoes. he does so as
if it's a real effort, as if there's no meaning
in shoes, laces, socks, feet, as if the entire world
is a distant and annoying little buzzing sound.

the guy who isn't depressed says: "jesus! you
are freaking me out here! let me do that, ok?"

the depressed guy leans back on the couch,
his hands by his side. "ok" he says.

very gently, the guy who isn't depressed unties
the depressed guy's shoe laces. then the
guy who isn't depressed pulls off the

depressed guy's shoes (adidas, track shoes).
then the guy who isn't depressed pulls
off the depressed guy's socks.

"wow!" says the guy who isn't depressed. "VERY nice.
you've even got sexy toes, did you know that?"

the depressed guy smiles just a tiny little
bit, but his lips barely move at all, actually.
you'd miss it if you weren't looking real real
close. the guy who isn't depressed IS looking
real real close. "that's better," says the
guy who isn't depressed. "i saw that little
tiny hint of a smile. i knew there was one
in there somewhere. now, stand up, ok?"

the depressed guy stands up real slow.

"that's it!" says the guy who isn't depressed.
"real good!! now i'm gonna undo your
belt and unzip your pants, ok?"
something dark and scary crosses the
depressed guy's face. then it fades, mostly.
"ok," says the depressed guy.

the guy who isn't depressed unbuckles the
depressed guy's belt, pulls down his zipper.

"you are one sexy guy," says the guy
who isn't depressed. "don't be alarmed
if i get a hardon, ok? it doesn't mean
we have to have sex. it only means
i'm standing here naked undressing
a very sexy guy who i happen to like
a whole lot. it's a natural reaction,
sorry."

"sure," says the depressed guy. "whatever."

the depressed guy really does not seem
to care about what is happening at this
moment. he really does not seem to care
that a naked and very attractive
big-dicked young man is undressing him.

"let's just get you undressed and
in bed beside me," says the guy
who isn't depressed. "then i'm gonna
do some serious holding and comforting,
no doubt about that."

"hmmm" says the depressed guy. there is
a tear at each corner of his
deep dark sexy brooding eyes.

the guy who isn't depressed pulls
down the depressed guy's pants, then
he pulls down the depressed guy's underpants.

"come on," says the guy who isn't
depressed. "step out of these, ok?
just lift your feet, and take a little
step. it's not that difficult."

the depressed guy obeys, as if why
the hell not, why the hell not bother,
why the hell not do anything, or
why DO anything, for that matter. the depressed
guys eye's are vacant, dark, almost
blank, actually, and just a bit scary.

the depressed guy is totally naked now,
and beautiful, and masculine, and very
very sexy.

so now both the depressed guy and
the guy who isn't depressed walk

naked down the hall into the depressed
guy's bedroom. in there is a
big bed, full-size, at least,
maybe bigger. the bed is neatly
made. the guy who isn't
depressed pulls back the covers.
the sheets look clean and smooth.

"come on" says the guy who isn't depressed.
"lie down here beside me, ok?"

the guy who isn't depressed climbs onto
the bed and lies down on his back.
the depressed guy lies down, too,
right beside him. they are both
lying on their backs. the guy who
isn't depressed pulls up the covers
and snuggles in beside the depressed
guy. he pushes his nose up against
the side of the depressed guy's neck,
drapes one arm over the depressed
guy's chest.

"any idea what's wrong?" says the
guy who isn't depressed. "or is
it the same as usual?"

the depressed guy sighs darkly.
"the same" he says. "i just get
this way sometimes. i thought
you understood."

"i do," says the guy who isn't
depressed. "really. it's like
a brain-wave thing or something. your
brain waves go one way for a while,
and then they go the other." he
kisses the depressed guy on the

side of his neck. "did i say it
right?"

"pretty much" says the depressed
guy.

"thought so," says the guy who isn't
depressed. "i'm a pretty good listener,
you know. i pay attention."

"hmmmmm," says the depressed guy, his
voice fading away, as
if he sort of doesn't care.

they lie there naked in bed together,
the guy who isn't depressed pressing
himself close up against the depressed
guy, cuddling, snuggling, gently
kissing the depressed guy's neck from time.

"i do love you," says the guy who
isn't depressed.

"and i love you," says the depressed guy.

"i'm sorry you're feeling down," says
the guy who isn't depressed. "i'm here
to help, and you won't feel bad forever. we
both know that."

"ummm," says the depressed guy. "we both
know."

they lie there naked together,
under the covers, and as the
guy who isn't depressed snuggles up
against the depressed guy, the
depressed guy starts to snuggle back,

just a little, but, still, there
is a bit of reciprocation going on.

they lie there like that a long time.
they both lose track. 2 hours?
3 hours? only the beside lamp
is on, and neither of them
gets out of bed to turn it off.
they both fall asleep.

in the middle of the night,
the guy who isn't depressed
is awakened by the
depressed guy speaking these words:

"climb on top of me, ok?"

the depressed guy is flat on his
back, looking up at the ceiling.

the guy who isn't depressed
rolls over, climbs on top of
the depressed guy. they push
their chests together. they
push their big dicks together.
they push their bellies together.
they kiss each other, hard.

"there," says the depressed guy.
"perfect. just stay this way, ok?"

the depressed guy has his arms
wrapped tightly around the back
of the guy who isn't depressed.
the depressed guy is holding,
hugging, pulling the guy who
isn't depressed tight up against
him. they both have big hardons now.

"this feels fantastic" says the
depressed guy. "let's just lie
here this way, the rest of the
night, ok?"

the guy who isn't depressed says:
"sure, whatever you want."

they lie there like that. the
bottoms of their
hard dicks are pressed tight up
against each other.

the depressed guy holds onto
the guy who isn't depressed
as if the
guy who isn't depressed is the only thing in
the entire world that's pure
and virtuous and beautiful, the only thing
that even matters at all.

the guy who isn't depressed
likes this feeling, likes
this feeling that he's really
needed, wanted. he likes this feeling
a lot. he likes it so much he
starts to cry. his
tears run down his face and plop
onto the face of the depressed
guy.

both guys are hot, and sweaty.
they can feel the liquid sheen
of the sweat between their chests,
pushed tightly against each other.

the guy who isn't depressed pushes
his arms under the back of the

depressed guy, and hugs him
as tightly as he can.

they lie there in bed in the
middle of the night, both crying now,
both hugging each other as hard
as they can, their big stiff dicks
pressed up against each other.

in another instant, they are
both crying and spurting their cum
all over each other's bellies,
at practically the exact same moment.

then they go limp, the guy who
isn't depressed slumping on top
of the guy who is; then, again,
they hug each other tight,
their arms wrapped around each
other; they kiss each other on
the neck. embracing, feeling
the heat of each other's bodies–
the embrace they are sharing
the balm, the salve, and the
glue that assures them both,
whenever there's any doubt,
of why they truly belong together.

after they wipe themselves off,
they snuggle in for the rest of
the night. they both sleep like babies,
and, in the morning, everything's
fine, just fine– maybe even
beautiful.

Carl Miller Daniels is 59 years old. He currently lives in ruggedly masculine Homerun, VA. His previous works include *Museum Quality Orgasm* (Future Tense Books; 1996) *Shy Boys at Home* (Chiron Review Press; 1999) and *Riot Act* (Chiron Review Press; 2010). *Gorilla Architecture* is his first full-length book. Daniels and his lover, Jon (aka "the sweetest man in the world"), have lived together for over 30 years.

The author gratefully acknowledges the following publications where some of these poems first appeared:

Asphodel Madness

Assaracus

Chiron Review

FRiGG Magazine

FUCK!

My Favorite Bullet

poetz.com

Rusty Truck

[sic] magazine

Strangeroad

Thieves Jargon

Underground Voices

Whisper & Scream Magazine

Zygote In My Coffee

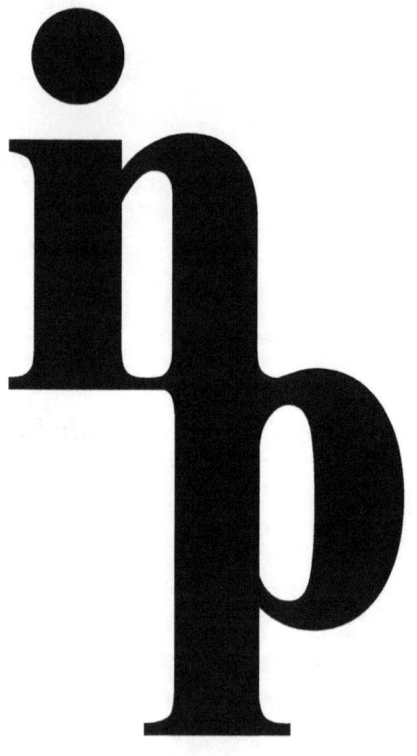

www.interiornoisepress.com

www.ingramcontent.com/pod-product-compliance
Lightning Source LLC
Chambersburg PA
CBHW020935090426
42736CB00010B/1146